Naturalizing Digital Immigrants

Naturalizing Digital Immigrants

The Power of Collegial Coaching for Technology Integration

Katie Alaniz and Dawn Wilson

ROWMAN & LITTLEFIELD
Lanham • Boulder • New York • London

Published by Rowman & Littlefield
A wholly owned subsidiary of The Rowman & Littlefield Publishing Group, Inc.
4501 Forbes Boulevard, Suite 200, Lanham, Maryland 20706
www.rowman.com

16 Carlisle Street, London W1D 3BT, United Kingdom

British Library Cataloguing in Publication Information Available

Library of Congress Cataloging-in-Publication Data

Alaniz, Katie.
Naturalizing digital immigrants : the power of collegial coaching for technology integration / Katie
Alaniz and Dawn Wilson.
pages cm
Includes bibliographical references and index.
ISBN 978-1-4758-1280-0 (hardcover)—ISBN 978-1-4758-1281-7 (pbk.)—
ISBN 978-1-4758-1282-4 (e-book)
1. Educational technology. 2. Adult education teachers—Training of. 3. Information technology. I.
Wilson, Dawn K. (Dawn Kathleen) II. Title.
LB1028.3.A4335 2015
371.33—dc23
2014048229

Contents

Acknowledgments

We, Katie and Dawn,
would like to express our heartfelt gratitude to our husbands,
Steven and Randy,
and to our families and friends
for consistently encouraging and supporting us
in fulfilling our lives' callings.

We would also like to thank
Dr. Linda Brupbacher, Miguel Guhlin, and Dr. Les Foltos
for their dedication to reading, reflecting upon, and offering feedback
through our process of completing this work.

We would be remiss not to extend our appreciation to
the many graduate students, teachers, and administrators
who so willingly and thoughtfully shared their coaching experiences,
thereby inspiring countless others with their passion for lifelong learning.

Finally, this book is dedicated to the glory of God.

Introduction

Whether read from the perspective of a school administrator, instructional technologist, or other individual seeking to assist teachers in more effectively mining the vast potential of instructional technology, this guidebook sheds light upon the immense promise of collegial coaching for expanding technology integration within school environments.

The book commences by acquainting the reader with the power of knowledge transfer between digital natives and digital immigrants. The term "digital immigrants" refers both to teachers not born in the digital age as well as those not comfortable using technology in the classroom. Such educators may lack the technological expertise necessary to provide technology-rich lessons for their students.

In this book, "digital immigrant" signifies less of a chronological label and more of an experiential label. For these individuals, a targeted intervention is needed to help them feel confident enough to integrate technology into their instruction, and collegial coaching from technology-savvy colleagues, or "digital natives," represents an effective strategy.

After examining the possibilities of knowledge transmission from digital natives to digital immigrants, coaching programs within educational settings are investigated, including an overview of the foundations of collegial coaching for technology integration. Collegial coaching programs have been recommended as an integral component of comprehensive professional development strategies for aiding teachers in meeting the demands of their occupation. An overview of the literature in support of this model is presented within this book.

The need for collegial coaching is subsequently assessed, and new dilemmas facing the digital immigrants guiding today's classrooms are highlighted. Challenged with escalating mandates for accountability, many educators of today consistently struggle to allocate time within their busy schedules to learn about the latest instructional technology, let alone identify the means by which to incorporate it into the required curriculum. Encouragement and assistance in doing so is needed now more than ever before.

The reader is then introduced to strategies for applying the basics of collegial coaching. More specifically, a proven model for effective coaching for technology integration is outlined. The methods presented have been employed in school settings for the past several years with great success, providing novice users of technological resources with enhanced confidence in utilizing such tools in their own planning and teaching.

Next, the book underscores the unique perspectives offered by digital natives within the field of education. Collegial coaching provides a professional helping relationship and process in which a coach with expertise and experience aids the learning and acquisition of new skills by a colleague. Such programs represent a professional development vehicle by which educators can learn to integrate technology with success. Strategies and techniques for cultivating quality coaches within school settings are provided.

Approaches to creating a collaborative learning environment in which teachers coach teachers are then described. Topics include expanding coaches' background knowledge and skills about technology integration, exploring principles for effective coaching, and providing structure and ongoing support of the coaching processes.

The reader is then offered practical steps for tackling teacher apprehension through the collegial coaching process. By way of following specific strategies for guiding coached teachers in finding success, collegial coaching programs pave the way for eliminating digital immigrants' apprehensions regarding technology integration.

The book concludes with a summative overview of methods for fostering an environment of collegial coaching within school settings. As coached teachers achieve developmental milestones, their enthusiasm often becomes contagious, thus inspiring them to share their successes with colleagues.

Also included are real-life success stories involving the transformation of teacher technology integration through collegial coaching, designed to inspire and inform readers in their journey to implement this strategy within their own professional settings. Such narratives serve to reaffirm the reality that an investment in coaching through successful technology integration holds the potential to profoundly and perpetually transform the culture of a school campus.

Chapter One

Bridging the Great Divide

Adaptability is about the powerful difference between adapting to cope and adapting to win.

—Max McKeown

In today's society, few would argue with the notion that technological innovation is transforming nearly every aspect of life. In fact, one might find difficulty pinpointing an area of day-to-day existence not in some sense impacted by ever-present and continuously morphing technological tools and resources. Quite positively, this perpetually intensifying deluge of technological innovation is changing the ways we view and experience the world. As the waves of technological advancement continue to surge, few environments are more impacted by their wake than the realms of education.

Within classroom settings, the promise of technology is immense. It holds the potential to enhance educational opportunities for learners across the globe. When implemented effectively, technology frequently enriches the extent and impact of skillfully executed teaching. It offers educators useful tools for reenvisioning the delivery of vital concepts, thereby enabling students to become cocreators of their own learning experiences.

From a practical standpoint, technological innovations often decrease costs while expanding the productivity of teachers and learners. Of course, none of this is possible unless classroom teachers are equipped to implement these innovative educational tools, and the challenge of reaching a point of technological expertise is an ever-moving target. This realization implies that if teachers are expected to keep pace, then a solid plan for ongoing, targeted, and differentiated professional development is required.

1

TECHNOLOGY INTEGRATION: WHAT'S THE BIG DEAL?

Ideally, time spent within school settings should equip students for the world of tomorrow, using the most innovative tools of today. Educators are charged with the task of applying real-world technology while guiding students as they tackle everyday problems. In doing so, teachers hold the potential to offer learners a competitive edge in an ever-changing global economy.

Indeed, the promises of technology within learning environments seem virtually boundless. Yet, unless educators are adequately equipped with the knowledge, hands-on experience, and confidence necessary to effectively employ such resources, the value of educational technology dissipates as quickly as a rescinding tide. Many of today's educators grapple with the distressing feeling of lagging behind the curve. Such teachers wrestle with the concern that they lack the capacity to prepare students for the 21st century.

The students of today are the first generation to grow up with the Internet and other "new technologies." Although sometimes labeled the "N Gen" for Net generation or "D Gen" for digital generation, the term more often associated with this generation is "digital natives." In regards to performing tasks or collaborating via technological tools, such students speak a language of their own.

Their means of interacting socially and living life in general often differ vastly from those of their teachers and parents. An assemblage of ever-changing technological tools represents a common facet of this generation's daily lives. Not only do many of these technologies allow individuals to communicate instantaneously, but they also provide access to a plethora of information sources from virtually any location, all through the push of a button or the tap of a screen.

This technological environment differs greatly from that in which their parents grew up, and their parents' generation includes many of today's educators. In contrast to the technology-rich formative years and daily lives of digital natives, such individuals, or "digital immigrants," have spent much of their lives functioning in a less technologically progressive world. Innovative technologies that seem commonplace in the here and now were either nonexistent or in their infancy through many seasoned teachers' developmental years.

The educational systems within today's world face a dilemma. What is the most effective strategy for engaging and instructing 21st-century learners? Why does the task of teaching today's generation seem to differ so greatly from generations of the past? Could it be that today's students are so different? If this is the case, what is it that makes them different? Such inquiries are legitimate concerns for teachers who desire to educationally impact their learners' lives.

THE QUEST FOR TECH-SAVVY TEACHERS

The use of technology to support learning via student-centered methods represents an imperative for teachers of today. An abundance of evidence demonstrates that such approaches hold the potential to positively influence student performance (Abramovich 2006; Lei and Zhao 2007). However, researchers have discovered that many teachers may not be implementing student-centered methods of technology integration because they lack the knowledge needed to do so (Kopcha 2008).

Educators who desire to provide a high-quality, technology-rich academic experience for their students may be unable to keep pace with constantly developing technological advancements for classrooms. Faced with increasing demands for accountability—including implementation of high-stakes assessments, more stringent regulations, and heightened curricular standards—many of today's teachers find themselves unable to set aside the time necessary to research the latest technological tools for educational use, let alone explore ways in which to incorporate them into the required curriculum (McCrary and Mazur 2010).

Preparation for required common assessments from state and national accountability mandates often consumes the school day, leaving little time for creative, student-centered, project-based learning with technology. Correlating compulsory standards and assessments with technology-rich projects is often difficult for teachers and requires more time than seemingly available. Teachers must learn to work and plan collaboratively using productivity technology tools in order to accomplish all of these planning, teaching, and assessment requirements.

Howland, Jonassen, and Marra (2012) suggest that meaningful learning requires tasks that are authentic, constructive, active, cooperative, and intentional. Furthermore, these characteristics of meaningful learning are distinctly interrelated. Instructional activities should support and engage a combination of learning tasks incorporating technology as a tool *with* which to learn, rather than *from* which to learn. Effective teachers must demonstrate knowledge of the content but also knowledge of pedagogy and technology, and teachers possessing this fusion of expertise are difficult to find.

A CULTURE OF PROFESSIONAL ISOLATION

The complexity and challenge of addressing such issues is intensified by the rising professional seclusion of classroom teachers, which represents one of the commonplaces of contemporary educational research (Zahorik 1987; Flinders 1988). Furthermore, modern school systems seem to suffer from a persistent failure to generate intentional, lasting change at the classroom level. Not surprisingly, these two phenomena are interconnected. As explained by Les Foltos, author of *Peer Coaching: Unlocking the Power of Collaboration* (2013), "Teachers work largely in isolation, so innovation doesn't spread from classroom to classroom" (Salsito 2013).

In many cases, classroom seclusion contributes to teachers' lack of confidence in their effectiveness as educators and anxiety surrounding professional appraisal. Additionally, heightened demands for accountability ultimately incite them to focus their energies inward, immersing themselves more deeply within their own classroom environments. Naturally, such mind-sets are often blamed for teachers' hesitancy to investigate and adopt alternative methods that require them to venture beyond their comfort zones (Hargreaves and Reynolds 1989).

In his book entitled *Schools that Change*, Lew Smith (2012) explains that in order to bring about change, school communities must acknowledge the culture and context of the school while encouraging conversations about students, teaching and learning, and vision and progress among teachers, administrators, and parents. Such conversations emancipate teachers from their islands of remoteness, serving as a constructive progression toward collegiality as well as providing crucial initial steps in promoting a more lasting sense of educational transformation.

THE RISING RELEVANCE OF COLLEGIAL COACHING PROGRAMS

The noticeable implications of teacher seclusion coupled with the surmounting necessity of 21st-century instruction have generated amplified attention to the merits of nontraditional strategies for professional development. When implemented effectively, such approaches unite teachers in hands-on, authentic working relationships with one another. An imperative focus among today's school administrators involves creating professional cultures more responsive and receptive to technological innovation and its implications.

One means of facilitating hands-on, authentic working relations among teachers is the process known as coaching. Several types of coaching models have existed within various realms of society for decades (Knight 2007). For example, in the business sector, executive coaching now represents a booming industry. Co-active coaching involves coaching a person beyond the borders of work to include various facets of his or her entire life. Cognitive coaching, first introduced by Costa and Garmston (2002), focuses on shifting an individual's perceptions and patterns of thought.

Many school districts employ literacy coaches to assist teachers in student reading goal achievement and implementation of literacy-focused strategies. Such instructional coaches typically occupy full-time professional development roles, working on-site in schools to support teachers in incorporating research-based teaching strategies (Knight 2007).

Collegial coaching differs from many other coaching models primarily in that it takes place between colleagues or peers (not someone with administrative and accountability authority). These programs have been recommended as an integral component of comprehensive professional development strategies. Such initiatives were found to effectively benefit teachers in meeting the demands of their occupation. In fact, researchers have discovered that the addition of a collegial coach in a similar field to that of the teacher is one of the most powerful predictors of educator retention (Smith and Ingersoll 2004).

Collegial coaching might be defined as a professional helping relationship between a "coach" who has experience in the role or concepts being learned by a colleague. The coach and coachee essentially "work together for a specific, predetermined purpose in order that professional performance can be improved as well as validated" (SDC Knowledge and Learning Processes Division 2007, 1). This process is one element of the more vast body of professional development that investigates methods by which educators learn to teach successfully.

The nonjudging and nonevaluative atmosphere of collegial coaching programs sets them apart from other formats designed for professional growth, such as more formalized teacher appraisal methods. Collegial coaching focuses on the collaborative sharing, refinement, and expansion of professional knowledge and skills. Currently, an array of collegial coaching terms and models exist throughout professional settings, and all of these models maintain a common goal—enhance professional practice through the collaboration of colleagues.

Statistical support for the advantages of collegial coaching is compelling. Dr. Bruce Joyce (1987), a notable pioneer in studies of coaching among educators, discovered the following:

- 5 percent of learners will transfer a new skill into their practice as a result of theory;
- 10 percent will transfer a new skill into their practice with theory and demonstration;
- 20 percent will transfer a new skill into their practice with theory, demonstration, and practice within the training;
- 25 percent will transfer a new skill into their practice with theory, demonstration, practice within the training, and feedback;
- 90 percent will transfer a new skill into their practice with theory, demonstration, practice within the training, feedback, and *coaching*.

Many of today's teachers lack the technological expertise necessary to provide technology-rich lessons for their students. A targeted intervention is needed to help these technically inexperienced teachers feel confident enough to integrate technology into their instruction, and collegial coaching from technology-savvy colleagues represents an effective strategy.

THE POWER OF KNOWLEDGE
TRANSFER BETWEEN COLLEAGUES

The potential power of knowledge transfer between such technologically-experienced digital native teachers and technologically-inexperienced digital immigrants is immense. Teachers who desire to effectively implement technology into their classrooms but are uncertain of the means by which to do so are superior candidates for a technology-focused collegial coaching program.

In fact, coaching directly addresses a number of typical barriers to technology incorporation within classroom settings. Researchers discovered that elementary teachers who began assimilating technology with the aid of a coach more readily overcame barriers to integration such as lack of time, technical issues, and integration of technology into a real-life classroom setting (Franklin, Turner, Kariuki, and Duran 2001). Strudler and Hearrington (2009) also reported that "educators are more likely to incorporate technology into their instruction when they have access to coaching and mentoring" (6).

Tennessee's EdTech Launch attempted to evaluate the effectiveness of technology in educational settings. This program provided teachers with technological resources, curricular materials, and technology coaches who offered them just-in-time, personalized support. Outcomes of the study showed heightened student engagement and enhanced utilization of technology by students in meaningful and intensive ways.

Additional studies have demonstrated the benefits of collegial coaching for technology integration among educators from all levels of instruction in both private and public school settings (Wilson, Brupbacher, Simpson, and Alaniz 2013; Wilson, Brupbacher, Merrin, and Woolrich 2013). Researchers found that collegial coaching bridged the divide for teachers. Coaches met with colleagues on their own campuses to deliver individualized, targeted, student-centered, and content appropriate technological interventions designed and implemented specifically for the teachers and students with great success.

Considering these implications, collegial coaching holds promise for effectively meeting the needs of teachers who desire to utilize technology to enhance student learning but lack the skills to do so (Kopcha 2008). Such coaching programs hold the potential to direct schools toward a scenario in which professional educators also view themselves as learners.

In these cases, learning is accomplished in partnerships, as colleagues collaborate in concert with one another, both through one-on-one formats and in small group settings. Rather than reluctantly attending off-site professional development workshops, teachers are granted the opportunity to join forces within their own school environments, thus providing a more genuine, authentic backdrop in which to learn and grow.

CONTEMPLATING COLLEGIAL COACHING'S MERITS OVER TRADITIONAL MODELS

Grunwald Associates (2010) surveyed one thousand teachers and found that those who utilize technology to facilitate teaching and learning realized greater benefits to student achievement, motivation, and time on task than those who spent less time incorporating technological tools. Surprisingly, however, only 34 percent of the teachers surveyed use technology more than 10 percent of the time in their classrooms. Such findings point to the fact that providing teachers with technology tools does not necessarily mean these resources will be effectively utilized to maximize student learning.

Within traditional professional development settings, an individual teacher frequently represents one audience member among countless others in attendance. Such workshops often address a wide range of topics, each of which may or may not pertain to the real-world classroom experiences of teachers and their students. The concepts presented may easily fall short of addressing their most pressing concerns in relation to their work as educators and goals for meeting learners' academic needs.

After a full day of sitting, listening, and note-taking, there exists an immense likelihood of teachers feeling inundated with a torrent of information. Upon return to their classrooms the next morning, notes they have taken only a day before may likely be tucked away—right along with the ideas and potential applications received at the workshop or conference. As teachers manage day-by-day job requirements, the lessons taught within traditional professional development settings (no matter how seemingly innovative or compelling at the time) drift from teachers' minds with the tide of daily existence, often never to be seen again.

Regrettably, most professional development opportunities seem detached from the classroom experience, thereby denying teachers the opportunity to immediately apply the concepts presented in meaningful ways. For teachers, as for their students, scaffolding within the framework of application is essential for bringing about effectual learning. Educators are consistently expected to differentiate instruction for their students. Shockingly, however, their own professional development experiences are largely one-size-fits-all and rarely customized to their individual instructional needs. These experiences are often perceived as "more of a burden than a help" (Knight 2007, 7).

Contrary to traditional off-site professional development experiences, coaching programs invite educators to collaborate with fellow colleagues at their exact points of need. Through the promotion of collaboration and the sharing of ideas, collegial coaching serves as an equalizing medium between coaches and coached teachers, thus altering their roles to some extent.

In such settings, coaches are not perceived as the "sage on the stage" or the sole experts and information providers. Instead, they take on more of a "guide on the side" role, serving as facilitators or partners for joint learning endeavors. In the words of Les Foltos, "Good coaches have the capability to help their peers improve teaching and learning." Moreover, "Successful coaches understand that they cannot take on the role of the expert. Rather than answering questions, [effective coaches] respond with questions that get [colleagues] to think more deeply about the issues" (Salcito 2013).

Collegial coaching programs encourage teachers to transition from the role of passive learners who attempt to mimic what they see and hear from the expert instructor. In doing so, they increasingly become participants and collaborators in the creation of knowledge. Often, in fact, both the coach and the coachee gain new knowledge and skills as they work together to plan instruction. Specific concerns and strategies for addressing issues are discussed and reflected upon in concert, with coaches and coached teachers working shoulder-to-shoulder.

The need for collaboration is paramount to instructional change, and the merits of developing this climate within school settings and fostering a capacity for change cannot be overemphasized. While coaching focuses on the integration of technology, the benefits of individualized coaching also mean that the best technological tools, pedagogy, and content are matched to implement the most effective instruction.

According to Beglau and colleagues (2011), when given the opportunity to receive professional development through coaching, teachers "develop confidence and effectiveness in designing and supporting technology-rich environments that maximize student learning" (3). In the authors' own work as coaches, participants consistently report remarkable change in teachers' efficacy as they collaborate one-on-one with fellow educators to plan and implement their ideas for technology use with students.

When teachers are provided the chance to apply their personal creativity and ideas for lesson planning while collaborating with a coach on their campus—rather than in an isolated professional development session—incentives and accountability for integration and implementation increase by leaps and bounds. In such scenarios, teachers ultimately find greater success.

In 2010 the National Education Technology Plan (NETP) acknowledged the need to leverage technology to improve learning and assessment. This same plan calls for connected teaching, in which teaching becomes a team endeavor that is collaborative, coherent, and continuous. These methods incorporate in-person professional growth opportunities and focus on immediate needs. Collegial coaching is the answer to NETP's proposal for connecting teachers and developing educators proficient at effectively leveraging the possibilities of instructional technology.

ESSENTIAL IDEAS TO REMEMBER

The power of knowledge transfer between digital natives and digital immigrants is immense, holding the potential to transform school environments in ways traditional professional development endeavors cannot. Currently, countless educators lack the technological expertise essential for developing and delivering technology-rich lessons to their students. These digital immigrant educators (regardless of chronological age) desperately need a targeted intervention to help them feel confident enough to integrate technology into their instruction, and collegial coaching from technology-savvy colleagues, or "digital natives," represents an effective strategy.

REFERENCES

Abramovich, S. "Early Algebra with Graphics Software as a Type II Application of Technology," *Computers in the Schools* 22(3–4) (2006): 21–33.
Beglau, M., J. C. Hare, L. Foltos, K. Gann, J. James, H. Jobe, J. Knight, and B. Smith. *Technology, Coaching, and Community.* (2011): Retrieved from www.iste.org/learn/coaching-white-paper.
Bullock, D. "Moving from Theory to Practice: An Examination of the Factors That Preservice Teachers Encounter as They Attempt to Gain Experience Teaching with Technology during Field Placement Experiences," *Journal of Technology and Teacher Education* 12(2) (2004): 211–237.
Flinders, D. J. "Teacher Isolation and the New Reform," *Journal of Curriculum and Supervision* 4(l) (1988): 17–29.
Foltos, L. J. *Peer Coaching: Unlocking the Power of Collaboration.* Thousand Oaks, CA: Corwin Press, 2013.
Franklin, T., S. Turner, M. Kariuki, and M. Duran. "Mentoring Overcomes Barriers to Technology Integration," *Journal of Computing in Teacher Education* 18(1) (2001): 26–31.
Grunwald Associates LLC. "Educators, Technology, and 21st Century Skills: Dispelling Five Myths: A Study on the Connection between K–12 Technology Use and 21st Century Skills." (2010): Retrieved from www.waldenu.edu/Documents/Degree-Programs/Full_Report_-_Dispelling_Five_Myths.pdf.
Hargreaves, A., and D. Reynolds. *Educational Policies: Controversies and Critiques.* Lewes: Falmer Press, 1989.
Howland, J., D. Jonassen, and R. Marra. *Meaningful Learning with Technology* (4th ed.). Boston: Pearson Education, 2012.
Joyce, B. Proceedings from *Staff Development Awareness Conference.* Columbia, SC: 1987.

Knight, J. *Instructional Coaching: A Partnership Approach to Improving Instruction.* Thousand Oaks, CA: Corwin Press, 2007.

Koehler, M. J., and P. Mishra. "What Is Technological Pedagogical Content Knowledge?" *Contemporary Issues in Technology and Teacher Education* 9(1) (2009): Retrieved from www.citejournal.org/vol9/iss1/general/article1.cfm.

Kopcha, T. "A Systems-Based Approach to Technology Integration Using Mentoring and Communities of Practice," *Educational Technology Research and Development* 58(2) (2010): 175–190.

Lei, J., and Y. Zhao. "Technology Uses and Student Achievement: A Longitudinal Study," *Computers and Education* 49 (2007): 284–296.

McCrary, N., and J. Mazur. "Conceptualizing a Narrative Simulation to Promote Dialogic Reflection: Using a Multiple Outcome Design to Engage Teacher Mentors," *Educational Technology Research and Development* 58(3) (2010): 325–342.

Salcito, A., "Unlock the Power of Collaboration through Peer Coaching—Les Foltos, USA," *Daily Edventures* (2013): Retrieved from www.dailyedventures.com/index.php/2013/03/20/lesfoltos/.

SDC Knowledge and Learning Processes Division. *SDC Knowledge Management Toolkit.* (2007): Retrieved from www.sdc-learningandnetworking.ch/en/Home/SDC_KM_Tools/media/SDC-KM-Toolkit/Collegial%20Coaching/06_Collegial%20Coaching_150dpi.pdf.

Smith, Lew. *Schools That Change: Evidence-Based Improvement and Effective Change Leadership.* Thousand Oaks, CA: Corwin Press, 2012.

Smith, T., and R. Ingersoll. "Reducing Teacher Turnover: What Are the Components of Effective Induction?" *American Educational Research Journal* 41 (2004): 198–214.

Strudler, N., and D. Hearrington. "Quality Support for ICT in Schools," *International Handbook of Information Technology in Primary and Secondary Education* (pp. 579–596). Springer US: 2008.

United States Department of Education, Office of Educational Technology. "National Educational Technology Plan." (2010): Retrieved from www.ed.gov/edblogs/technology/netp-2010/.

Wilson, D., L. Brupbacher, C. Simpson, and K. Alaniz. "Naturalizing Digital Immigrants: Technology Integration and Implications for Teacher Professional Development," *Texas Study of Secondary Education* 22(2) (2013): 36–40.

Wilson, D., L. Brupbacher, C. Simpson, R. Merren, and R. Woolrich. "Making Disciples: The Effects of Technology Integration Coaching," *The International Christian Community for Teacher Education* 8(1) (2013).

Zahorik. J. A. "Teachers' Collegial Interaction: An Exploratory Study," *The Elementary School Journal* 87 (1987): 385–396.

Chapter Two

Investigating Coaching Programs within Educational Settings

Coming together is a beginning. Keeping together is progress. Working together is success.

—Henry Ford

As indicated within chapter 1, the professional development opportunities available to educators have historically involved some sense of isolation and irrelevancy. In the case of such traditional models, teachers typically find themselves subject to and reliant upon the agendas and viewpoints of outside "experts" (Sandholtz 1999). These sessions are often generically designed to meet the needs of many attendees, and as a result, they tend to effectively serve only a handful of participants.

Alternatively, coaching actively engages educators in reflecting upon their current and immediate teaching practices, and it encourages participants to become manufacturers of their own pertinent knowledge. Ultimately, coaching as a professional development model acknowledges the significance of a teacher's individualized needs and responsibilities within the realms of an educational setting, while maximizing learning for both the students and the professional.

THE COMMONPLACE OF INDIVIDUALISM WITHIN SCHOOL SETTINGS

Undoubtedly, the art of teaching represents a highly complex undertaking. Researchers estimate that within the course of a school day, educators typically make in excess of three thousand nontrivial decisions. Others call the practice of teaching a "wicked problem" within an ill-structured, highly complex, and ever-changing environment. The profession of teaching requires educators to integrate their understanding of student thinking and learning, their expertise of subject matter, and methods for communicating and transmitting their subject matter knowledge—all while integrating changing technology.

In spite of the intricacy involved in daily functioning, teaching is frequently viewed as a highly individualistic profession. The processes of formulating decisions and problem solving are often conducted in isolation, and collaboration with peers is typically limited. Furthermore, on those rare occasions in which collaboration does take place, interaction is frequently relegated to an interchange of everyday anecdotes or the sharing of tips and tricks for enhancing lessons (Hargreaves and Daw 1990).

In cases when teachers actually contemplate change in their professional practices, they typically garner advice from off-site "experts" through district in-service workshops or promptings from administrative directives. Although the implementation of such professional development—whether voluntary or mandatory—may be well intentioned, influence is often limited. Their one-size-fits-all design limits their potential for change, especially considering their detachment from day-to-day classroom events and circumstances. Thus, these training endeavors often do not impact classroom teachers in any substantial or enduring sense.

Educators naturally experience difficulty in applying models and strategies disconnected from their classroom environments. The passive role forced upon them through traditional methods of professional development is among the most significant shortcomings of such strategies. Moreover, these professional development experiences seldom provide teachers with opportunities to work collaboratively with fellow colleagues to personalize implementation efforts.

THE IMPLICATIONS OF MEANINGFUL COLLABORATION

Genuine, impactful collaboration involves both equity and reciprocal contribution between individuals. The task of transitioning from inconsequential professional development experiences to truly meaningful opportunities for authentic reflection and growth requires the active investment and participation of educators. Effective professional development grants teachers an increasingly involved role in their own learning. These meaningful professional development opportunities must incorporate the perspectives and voices of educators within their own school and classroom environments.

Many researchers have examined the effect of teachers' personal knowledge and its impact on their reasoning and decision-making abilities (Elbaz

1983; Clandinin 1986; Connelly and Clandinin 1988). Researchers consistently note the value of intrinsic trustworthiness of teachers' experiential knowledge. Such studies highlight educators' aptitude for selecting judicious courses of action within ever-fluctuating, often unpredictable classroom settings.

Although formerly dismissed as nothing more than unsophisticated experience fumbling around in the wake of scholarly philosophies, more recent research efforts have ascribed greater value to the daily work of educators. The art of teaching is now expressed in such terms as "personal practical knowledge," or a "moral, affective, and aesthetic way of knowing life's educational situations" (Connelly and Clandinin 1988) and "educator creativity" (Woods 1988, 59). Investigations of teacher knowledge impart educators' voices with increased strength, particularly within the realms of academic research and professional development, thus acknowledging the complexity of their calling.

These research insights entail significant implications for professional development approaches. They advocate for movement away from trainings that target educators in isolation. Nontraditional professional development endeavors seek to heighten teachers' ability to engage in deeper modes of reflection both personally and with colleagues.

Enabling educators to take part in on-site experiences such as coaching for technology integration provides teachers with the opportunity to unite with colleagues in collaborative interaction. In doing so, these encounters intuitively allow teachers' unique abilities, experiences, and insights to rise to the surface, thereby providing an impetus for sharing them with others. Professional development of this nature implies a transition from isolated, individual modes of training to collective, community experiences.

In the coaching internships led by Dawn, master's level technology students worked alongside three colleagues to assist them in integrating technology into their own professional practice. As part of that process, participants kept journals and assessed the progress. Each semester, nearly every coached teacher alluded to the benefits of collaboration with an on-campus colleague as they worked to facilitate technology into their classrooms. Some highlighted brainstorming benefits, and others appreciated the in-class, on demand assistance they received as they explored unfamiliar tools and resources.

Among the unique challenges technology integration brings is a fear of the unknown. A teacher can easily observe as a trainer applies technological tools in an off-site professional development session, but this does not necessarily mean that the same teacher will be prepared to return to the classroom and replicate its use.

All sorts of mishaps can occur during implementation. An Internet site may be blocked on the school network (even though it worked perfectly at home), or the plug-ins that enable a certain video to play may not be loaded, or the wrong version of Java may inhibit a program from functioning properly. A limitless number of unknowns threaten to hinder novice technology users from venturing beyond their comfort zones to try new things. Yet when a coach is present to scaffold the implementation, fears of unknown "tech failures" seem to diminish. Nathan, one of Dawn's interns, remarked,

> My coachee was enthusiastic about the coaching process. She was hesitant to engage students with technology because she was uncomfortable with the technology. While she knew administrators or others would help her if she requested, she didn't want to inconvenience anyone or take up their time. Through the coaching process, she was exposed to technology in a safe environment, building the confidence to try things she never would have previously considered. This confidence came because a person was dedicated to helping her with her needs. Without the coach, there would be no growth.

THE ROLE OF REFLECTIVE PRACTICE IN PROFESSIONAL DEVELOPMENT ENDEAVORS

Such notions of nontraditional professional development closely relate to the imperative of reflective practice. The principles of application, collaboration, and contemplation compose the foundation of professional development endeavors involving genuine reflection. Furthermore, such experiences acknowledge the unique and complex methods of reasoning expressed through professional action, and the strategies for transferring experience and expertise from one colleague to another.

Foundational conceptions of reflection rest in Dewey's (1933) interpretation of reflective reasoning as a critical tool for facilitating educators' organization of activities and development of effective courses of action with proper outcomes in sight. More specifically, he characterized reflective cognition as the "active, persistent, and careful consideration of any belief or supposed form of knowledge in the light of the grounds that support it and the further conclusions to which it tends" (9).

Dewey classified genuine reflection as that which transforms human behaviors from mere impulses to rational acts. Whereas nonreflective instruction may be described as routine, automatic, and limited, educators who use reflection venture beyond a demonstration of teaching behaviors shaped and stipulated by others. Furthermore, they discern issues, explore ideas, consider novel strategies, contemplate opportunities, and generate relevant encounters in learning to the benefit of their students.

The integration of reflection into teaching methods shows great promise for improving professional practice, and when that reflection takes place in collaboration with another professional, the outcome often develops into a rich learning experience. Currently, the number of educational institutions utilizing models of instructional coaching is mounting at an astounding rate.

In Knight's words (2006), "Coaching is becoming popular, in part, because many educational leaders recognize that the old form of professional development, built around traditional in-service sessions for teachers, simply doesn't affect student achievement" (36). Therefore, the impact of teachers' interactions with other educators in a true-to-life classroom setting remains a vital consideration in planning for professional growth experiences.

Reflection regarding successes, failures, connections, improvements, extensions, and the like all work together to improve one's teaching practice. Furthermore, feedback from a nonthreatening colleague holds the potential to make these reflective moments even more powerful. Educators benefit from opportunities to practice vital technological competencies "under good conditions and get help in the form of instruction, supervision, and feedback" (Siedentop and Tannehill 2000, 3).

EXTENDING THE CONCEPT OF "LEARNING BY DOING"

Quite possibly, there exists no name more frequently referenced throughout research regarding reflective practice and pedagogical advancement than that of Donald Schön (1983, 1987). Expounding upon the work of Dewey, Schön extends the concept of learning by doing through proposing a pedagogical epistemology that positions technical problem solving endeavors within the more general framework of reflective inquiry.

Schön contends that professional development has traditionally placed too great an emphasis on scientific theories and the suggestion that identifying solutions to problems might be accomplished in a clear-cut manner. Thus, off-site, detached training approaches frequently fall short of equipping teachers with the proficiencies required to manage the unforeseen and demanding occurrences they will certainly confront in the "real" world, or what Schön (1983) refers to as the "swampy lowlands" (3).

In Schön's viewpoint, "reflection-in-action" represents the capacity to reflect prior to a circumstance in which clear-cut solutions and scientific models are irrelevant. Reflection-on-action involves a process of reflecting upon the incident subsequent to the fact. Ultimately, both activities that require reflection previous to reaction in circumstances in which a definitive solution may not be apparent (reflection-in-action) as well as those that entail thoughtful reflection subsequent to action (reflection-on-action) comprise a necessary component of effective professional development endeavors.

Collegial coaching enables the coach and coachee to practice both reflection-in-action and reflection-on-action as they collaboratively reflect upon integrating new concepts still fresh on their minds during and subsequent to teaching. Coaching that includes such reflective activities serves to cultivate and enrich reflection as professional practice throughout the course of one's teaching career.

THE ADVENT OF COACHING WITHIN SCHOOL SETTINGS

Interestingly, extensive and formalized endeavors to evaluate professional development within educational settings were launched only within the last half of the 20th century. In their research, Showers and Joyce (1996) offer a systematic overview of the evolution of such professional development efforts and, more specifically, the introduction of formal coaching programs.

Initial endeavors to improve education in the mid-1950s primarily targeted academic quality and social egalitarianism. Early evaluations of faculty development strategies revealed that only a meager number of participants— possibly as few as 10 percent—effectively implemented the concepts presented within day-to-day teaching practices and curriculum development efforts. Incredulously, rates of transfer appeared even poorer for volunteers at such trainings.

Though well researched, the teaching strategies and curriculum-building methods exhibited at traditional professional development experiences fell short of bringing meaningful change in educators' everyday practices. Consequently, such training efforts failed to render significant impacts upon students' learning.

A lack of conclusive evidence regarding the ways in which educators learn novel teaching strategies and the means by which schools effectively circulate such techniques propagate the chasm between professional development experiences and meaningful transformation. Furthermore, the typical school calendar's structure encourages the scheduling of professional development trainings during the weeks of summer vacation. Meager results from these endeavors were blamed on teachers' lack of enthusiasm and poor attitudes, instead of examining faults within the structural underpinnings of these trainings.

Educational researchers and leaders began to more widely acknowledge that such movements rarely produced meaningful transformation, regardless of the amount of funding and public acceptance they garnered. Influenced by Vygotsky's (1978) notion of development as a social process and Bandura's (1971) ideas of social learning, literature of the 1970s increasingly acknowledged the social nature of teacher learning. Thus, educational research during this time highlighted the potential merits of collegial coaching with increasing frequency.

More specifically, the work of Vygotsky maintains that discussion among individuals provides a catalyst by which to generate meaning. In the course of such dialogue, teachers dynamically learn from and alongside one another. Likewise, in collegial coaching relationships, the process of collaboration encourages teachers to more effectively unravel and adopt novel concepts.

Furthermore, Bandura's research offers foundational insights pertaining to the implications of collegial coaching for social learning. The principle of social learning recognizes that individuals learn vicariously from one another by witnessing others' actions and perceiving associated corollaries. In this sense, collegial coaching also emphasizes the vital function of reciprocal learning.

By the early 1980s, researchers began to suppose that alterations to the organization of school settings and models of professional development might assist in the transfer of knowledge from theoretical assumptions to day-to-day practice. Additionally, the thought of attributing blame to teachers for the failings of traditional training endeavors began to seem increasingly unwarranted.

Interestingly, through interviews with more than 150 teachers across the United States, Knight (2007) discovered that teachers seldom actually resist change. More often, they resist poorly designed change initiatives. Teachers are bombarded with what Fullan and Hargreaves (1996) call "pressing immediacy," constantly facing papers to grade, parents to call, data to collect and analyze, and lessons to plan—not to mention classes to teach!

Rather than lacking the desire to implement fresh ideas or instructional tools, many educators' hesitancy to incorporate novel instructional strategies arises from the thought that planning and teaching concepts in a new way requires a great deal of additional planning time. For teachers, finding the extra time to do so often presents a tremendous challenge. However, when paired with a collegial coach, the workload related to planning can be shared, and accountability for actually implementing the new technology tool is increased.

Amazingly, the National Staff Development Council (2009) reported that over the course of the past decade, more than 90 percent of teachers participated in a traditional professional development session. Such sessions typically consisted of training offered off-site in a centralized location with a number of other teachers. Usually, these sessions last less than sixteen hours. Unfortunately, the majority of teachers attending such sessions reported feeling dissatisfied with their experiences.

The same study also found that professional development lasting less than fourteen hours often fails to render any impact on student learning or achievement outcomes (Darling-Hammond, Wei, Andree, Richardson, and Orphanos 2009). These discoveries again emphasize the need for long-term, ongoing, individualized coaching as opposed to homogeneously planned professional development.

The concept of coaching first introduced by Joyce and Showers (1980) found its basis in an extensive review of literature relating to the types of training most likely to bring about meaningful change. The training components addressed in their original work entailed theory presentation, modeling, practice, structured and open-ended feedback, and in-class assistance with transfer. Joyce and Showers postulated that teachers attempting to add new approaches to their professional repertoire would require frequent technical assistance within their classroom learning environments.

Their early research entailed a formal investigation and confirmation of the hypothesis that coaching, subsequent to preliminary training, would eventually lead to more effective transmittal of concepts than training in isolation (Showers 1982, 1984). Initial studies conclusively revealed that teachers who participated in coaching programs implemented novel teaching practices more frequently and applicably than did peers who sought to enhance their teaching practices in isolation.

Collegial coaching participants demonstrated expanded recollection of new techniques and more relevant application of such strategies over extended periods of time (Baker and Showers 1984). These findings suggest more technology integration might be possible when training is coupled with coaching. Interestingly, there currently exists very little research focusing upon this targeted type of instructional coaching by peers.

AN EXPANDING FORM OF PROFESSIONAL GROWTH

Coaching represents an expanding form of collaborative professional development among today's school environments. Within their research regarding the nature and implications of collaborative professional development, Valencia and Killion (1988) describe coaching as "the process where teams of teachers regularly observe one another and provide support, companionship, feedback, and assistance" (170). Although collegial coaching originated in K–12 educational settings, even within postsecondary environments, the number of thriving collegial coaching programs has multiplied over time.

As opposed to the coaching model, the archetypal process prescribed to teachers for augmenting their professional practice entails attendance at a workshop session or faculty development presentation, followed by self-directed application. When teachers attempt to apply technology practices presented at trainings, technology-related hurdles such as software and hardware incompatibilities, plug-in requirements, and system differences sometimes magnify challenges.

Teachers who experience collegial coaching from a peer with technology expertise demonstrate a nearly 90 percent implementation rate (Hargreaves and Daw 1990). Teachers participating in coaching opportunities (a) practice the novel techniques with greater frequency and acquire additional skills; (b) incorporate innovative strategies more aptly; (c) apply these newfound techniques repeatedly over time; and (d) discuss the reasoning behind their teaching strategies with students in order to assist their learners in understanding the associated purposes for implementation and expected classroom behaviors.

Initial conceptual investigations of collegial coaching portray a voluntary, confidential, and nonevaluative framework serving to mutually benefit two educators with comparable experiences (Joyce and Showers 1980). Within early research, the structure of collegial coaching frequently necessitated that teachers take part in equivalent professional development activities and formulate self-set goals for applying their new knowledge to classroom practices. Consequentially, both educators were concurrently involved in refining their teaching strategies.

Although collegial coaching began as a professional development method involving equivalent partners, within recent years, styles of coaching have expanded to include reciprocal coaching, expert coaching, interdisciplinary coaching, and intradisciplinary coaching.

This book specifically focuses on coaching relationships that exist between two equivalent partners—both of whom may be excellent educators—but the coach has superior technological expertise. Specifics to this coaching paradigm also include a focused goal of matching not only the right technology tool for the lesson but also on increasing student-centered teaching and student achievement.

Collegial coaching, first and foremost, establishes relationships. When implemented effectively, the coach essentially serves as a one-person support team for the teacher. The coached teacher is given close and continuing attention, and both the coach and coachee experience fresh ideas and viewpoints on the issue of reform. This added component allows educators within a school campus to reimagine, redesign, and renew their practice in ways that innovate and improve the quality of instruction and student achievement.

Within the forthcoming chapters, these methods of collegial coaching will be examined in greater depth, specifically in light of the unique facets of coaching for technology integration. Additionally, readers will discover strategies for determining how to best meet the specific needs of particular educators within varying school settings through coaching. The complexities associated with a plethora of teacher skill levels and experiences amidst a world of ever-evolving technological advances necessitate special considerations in designing effective coaching programs for technology integration.

ESSENTIAL IDEAS TO REMEMBER

Collegial coaching programs have been recommended as an integral part of comprehensive professional development strategies for aiding teachers in meeting the demands of their occupation. The variety of research in support of this model points to the effectiveness of collegial coaching programs for heightening teachers' professional learning experiences, ultimately leading to enhanced student learning and achievement.

In this chapter and throughout the remainder of the book, readers will recognize an overarching theme. Namely, no matter the form of collegial coaching adopted, the process must ultimately serve "to build communities of teachers who continually engage in the study of their craft" (Showers 1985, 43). Though sometimes donning varying structures, collegial coaching exemplifies an effective model for sustaining applicable and transformative professional development for teachers.

REFERENCES

Baker, R. G., and B. Showers. *The Effects of a Coaching Strategy on Teachers' Transfer of Training to Classroom Practice: A Six-Month Follow-Up Study.* New Orleans: American Educational Research Association, 1984.

Bandura, A. J. *Social Learning Theory.* New York: General Learning Press, 1971.

Clandinin, J. *Classroom Practice: Teacher Images in Action.* Lewes: Falmer Press, 1986.

Connelly, M., and J. Clandinin. *Teachers as Curriculum Planners: Narratives of Experience.* New York: Teachers' College Press, 1988.

Darling-Hammond, L., R. C. Wei, A. Andree, N. Richardson, and S. Orphanos. *Professional Learning in the Learning Profession: A Status Report on Teacher Development in the United States and Abroad.* (2009): Retrieved from www.learningforward.org/docs/pdf/nsdcstudy2009.pdf.

Dewey, J. *How We Think: A Restatement of the Relation of Reflective Thinking to the Educative Process.* Chicago: D.C. Heath, 1933.

Elbaz, F. *Teacher Thinking: A Study of Practical Knowledge.* London: Croom Helm, 1983.

Fullan, M., and A. Hargreaves. *What's Worth Fighting for in Your School?* New York: Teachers College Press, 1996.

Hargreaves, A., and R. Daw. "Paths of Professional Development: Contrived Congeniality, Collaborative Culture, and the Case of Peer Coaching," *Teaching and Teacher Education* 6 (1990): 227–241.

Joyce, B., and B. Showers. "Improving Inservice Training: The Messages of Research," *Educational Leadership* 37(5) (1980): 379–385.

Knight, J. "Instructional Coaching." *School Administrator* 63(4) (2006): 36–40.

———. *Instructional Coaching: A Partnership Approach to Improving Instruction.* Thousand Oaks, CA: Corwin Press, 2007.

Lortie, D. *School-Teacher: A Sociological Study.* Chicago: University of Chicago Press, 1975.

Sandholtz, J. H. *A Companion of Direct and Indirect Professional Development Activities.* Paper presented at the annual meeting of the American Educational Research Association, Montreal, Canada, 1999.

Schön, D. A. *The Reflective Practitioner: How Professionals Think in Action.* New York: Basic Books, 1983.

———. *Educating the Reflective Practitioner.* San Francisco: Jossey-Bass, 1987.

Showers, B. *Transfer of Training: The Contribution of Coaching.* Eugene, OR: Center for Educational Policy and Management, 1982.

———. *Peer Coaching: Strategy for Facilitating Transfer of Training.* Eugene, OR: Center for Educational Policy and Management, 1984.

———. "Teachers Coaching Teachers," *Educational Leadership* 43 (1985): 43–48.

Showers, B., and B. Joyce. "The Evolution of Peer Coaching," *Educational Leadership* 53 (1996): 12–16.

Siedentop, D., and D. Tannehill. *Developing Teaching Skills in Physical Education* (4th ed.). Mountain View, CA: Mayfield, 2000.

Skinner, M. E., and F. W. Welch. *Peer Coaching: Colleagues Helping Colleagues to Become Better Teachers.* Arizona State University, Tempe: International Society for Exploring Teaching Alternatives (ISETA) Annual Conference, 1994.

Valencia, S. W., and J. P. Killion. "Overcoming Obstacles to Teacher Change: Direction from School-Based Efforts," *Journal of Staff Development* 9(2) (1988): 168–174.

Vygotsky, L. *Mind in Society.* Cambridge, MA: Harvard University Press, 1978.

Webb, J. L., and K. McEnerney. *The View from the Back of the Classroom: Teacher Observation/Peer Support Program (TOPS).* Arizona State University, Tempe: International Society for Exploring Teaching Alternatives (ISETA) Conference, 1994.

Chapter Three

Assessing the Need for Technology Integration Coaching

A manager is a title; it does not guarantee success. Coaching is an action, not a title, and actions will result in successes!

—Catherine Pulsifer, *Words of Wisdom*

In today's digital age, educators face new dilemmas once never before imagined or anticipated by previous generations of teachers. Students' lives brim with technology, offering them mobile access to information and resources at an unprecedented rate. Perpetual digital connectivity enables them to generate multimedia content and share it with people across the globe in an instant.

Online social networks empower today's learners to communicate with others from all over the world, giving them a greater audience than ever before with whom to impart ideas, collaborate, and learn. Beyond the bounds of their school buildings, students experience nearly limitless freedom to pursue their passions, in their chosen ways and at their desired pace. For many of today's youth, technological advances are synonymous with infinite and instantaneous opportunity.

THE PROMISES AND PITFALLS OF TECHNOLOGICAL INNOVATION

Within these increasingly technologically infused times, the glaring challenge for educational systems involves leveraging modern technology to generate engaging, applicable, and individualized learning experiences for every student. Such learning encounters should mirror students' day-to-day lives while effectively preparing them for future opportunities and pursuits.

When compared to more traditional modes of classroom instruction, a pedagogical paradigm shift is required. In today's world of education, there exists an increasing demand for a transfer from teacher-centered to student-centered learning environments. Technological resources, when implemented effectively, enable teachers to position students at the focal point, empowering them to direct the course of their own learning by offering increased flexibility and room for creativity.

The results of a 2013 Pew Research Center survey involving nearly 2,500 Advanced Placement (AP) and National Writing Project (NWP) teachers indicate that educators perceive digital technologies to have benefitted them in instructing their middle school and high school students in a variety of ways (Purcell, Heaps, Buchanan, and Friedrich 2013). Ninety-two percent of these teachers report that the Internet has made a "major impact" on their ability to access content, resources, and materials for their teaching.

In that same study, nearly 70 percent of surveyed AP teachers perceive that the Internet has significantly affected their capacity to collaborate with other teachers through sharing ideas, and nearly the same number report that online access has considerably impacted their communication with parents. Finally, 57 percent of the teachers surveyed believe that the Internet has generated a sizable influence upon their interactions with students.

At the same time, however, many teachers feel that the Internet, mobile devices, and social media bring with them an assortment of new and unfamiliar challenges. In fact, 75 percent of the teachers surveyed believe that the Internet and other technological tools have placed a variety of additional demands on their professional practice. More specifically, they feel that such resources broaden the scope of content and skill areas in which they must become/remain proficient. Furthermore, 41 percent of the teachers surveyed perceive that such technological advances require more work from them in order to be effective educators.

Additionally, there exist clear generational differences among teachers in terms of their comfort levels with technology and its implementation in their classrooms. Reflecting the status quo in the general adult population, variances in technology use appear between older and younger educators. More specifically, while 64 percent of teachers below 35 years of age view themselves as "very confident" in using novel digital technologies, only 44 percent of those 55 or older maintain the same confidence levels regarding technology usage.

Not surprisingly, younger teachers generally demonstrate a greater likelihood of guiding students in developing or sharing work on a website, blog, or wiki. Furthermore, younger teachers are more likely than their more seasoned colleagues to encourage students to participate in online discussions and utilize collaborative web-based tools such as Google Docs to edit assignments. Additionally, younger teachers are more prone to collaborate with fellow educators on ideas for technology integration into instructional practice—22 percent of teachers under age 35 in comparison to 13 percent of teachers over age 55 (Pew 2013).

In the present day and age, technology is considered by the majority of educators and parents to comprise an integral component of providing a high-quality education (Ertmer 2005). But if this is the case, why isn't there an upsurge in technology integration in recent years? Although countless teachers are ready and willing to incorporate technology into instruction, certain barriers seem to inhibit full implementation.

Challenged with escalating mandates for accountability, many educators of today consistently struggle to allocate time within their busy schedules to learn about the latest instructional technology, let alone identify the means by which to incorporate it into the required curriculum. Encouragement and assistance in doing so is needed now more than ever before.

Ertmer and colleagues (2003) identified two categories into which such barriers might fall: extrinsic (first-order) and intrinsic (second-order). Extrinsic barriers include lack of resources, adequate training, technical support, and time. Intrinsic barriers involve teachers' beliefs, visions of technology integration, and levels of confidence. While these barriers are real, they can be effectively addressed through reflective collaboration and meaningful learning experiences with technology integration alongside a fellow educator.

TOUCHSTONES OF 21ST-CENTURY LEARNING

As technological innovation and integration continue to expand within our society, it grows increasingly imperative that teachers be prepared to develop and implement the skills and practices of digital age professionals. Moving onward, forward-thinking educators will progressively embrace instructional technology's potential to enhance their endeavors as co-learners with students and colleagues across the globe.

In today's digital age, simply being capable of utilizing technology is no longer enough. Teachers of the 21st century must proficiently guide their students in employing technology to investigate, discover, and demonstrate understanding. By integrating real-world technological tools into classroom lessons, teachers hold the potential to generate learning experiences that encourage students to grapple with real-world issues. Such opportunities prepare learners to be more meaningfully engaged in future endeavors, both as students in the classroom and eventually as professionals in the workplace.

ESSENTIAL SKILLS AND KNOWLEDGE IN THE DIGITAL AGE

Creativity and Innovation

The International Society for Technology in Education (ISTE) provides a set of standards for evaluating the skills and knowledge essential for students to effectively learn and productively contribute to a global and digital world. Not surprisingly, creativity and innovation rank at the top of this list. More specifically, students of the 21st century should be prepared to "demonstrate creative thinking, construct knowledge, and develop innovative products and processes using technology" (ISTE 2007).

The value of fostering creativity and innovation is undeniable, and technological advancements have produced a plethora of unique tools useful for enhancing this process. Yet in a world in which many teachers face schedules filled to capacity and increasingly scripted curriculum frameworks, how often are they afforded the opportunity to create and innovate in their own lives? How frequently are they encouraged to invent something new to solve a problem within their classrooms?

Many educators' days are so consumed with covering the required curriculum and preparing students for standardized assessments that few moments remain for genuinely imaginative and inventive endeavors. When such concepts seem foreign to their day-to-day practices, it is particularly difficult to imagine how teachers might utilize technological tools in the classroom to spark students' creativity and innovation.

Communication and Collaboration

According to ISTE (2007), the second set of skills paramount to creating 21st-century learning opportunities centers on communication and collaboration. More specifically, students should be proficient at "using digital media and environments to communicate and work collaboratively, including at a distance, to support individual learning and contribute to the learning of others" (ISTE 2007).

With each passing day, cutting-edge technological tools and resources surface for enhancing our ability to communicate with others—whether a colleague in the classroom next door or a new acquaintance halfway around the world. Whereas collaboration was once limited to the times and places in which participants could be physically present, individuals are now able to collaborate at all hours of the day and in any location, regardless of geographical whereabouts and time zones.

Webster-Smith, Albritton, and Kohler-Evans (2012) remarked, "People in organizations unknowingly cry out for meaningful conversations that are positive, fruitful, and constructive. The significance of meaningful conversations is especially critical in schools where administrators and teachers are either working in isolation or at cross-purposes" (xii). Just as teaching professionals "cry out" for opportunities to meaningfully converse and collaborate with other dedicated educators, today's students desire to establish points of connection with one another and to work together in various learning endeavors.

We live in an increasingly fast-paced world in which people often find themselves drawn toward the "path of least resistance," feeling compelled to relentlessly accomplish the greatest amount of work in the least amount of time. Such pursuits often implicate a sense of isolationism, requiring one to separate from others in order to more efficiently check task after task off their to-do lists. Although increased technology use is often associated by digital immigrants with a heightened sense of remoteness, technological innovation can also serve as a tool for enhancing communication and collaboration among educators and students.

Innovative digital tools and resources are emerging that will enable teachers and students to interact, team up, and publish with peers and experts, both within and beyond the boundaries of the school yard. When incorporated effectively, such technologies encourage learners to develop enriched communication skills as they convey information and ideas to various audiences using an assortment of formats. Additionally, through these experiences, students receive the opportunity to engage with learners from other cultural backgrounds, thus fostering deepened cultural understanding and global awareness.

Students of the 21st century are eager to interact, work together, and learn from one another—whether within their own classrooms and schools or across countries and continents. Yet unless today's teachers remain in touch with the latest technologies for communication and collaboration, in addition to more student-centered pedagogies, they will struggle with devising opportunities for incorporating them into the curriculum. Without encouragement and guidance in doing so, it seems doubtful that teachers who seldom use such technology in their own lives will creatively tap into its potential with their students.

Research and Information Fluency

The third set of ISTE (2007) standards involves students' abilities to "apply digital tools to gather, evaluate, and use information." More explicitly, students are expected to design strategies for guiding their quests for new information. Furthermore, they should be able to organize, investigate, assess, synthesize, and research from a range of sources and media. Students of the 21st century must also be skilled at evaluating and selecting information sources and digital resources based on the task at hand. Finally, students are expected to interpret data and report their findings.

In a world in which sources of information—whether trustworthy and useful or misleading and inadequate—may be found in abundance with the click of a button or tap of a screen, the importance of developing research and information fluency cannot be overemphasized. Anyone with Internet access seldom encounters a shortage of information. On the contrary, students of today are frequently bombarded with too much rather than too little data. Thus, the challenge comes in deciphering how best to utilize the information at hand as well as in knowing which data to discard.

As more and more information becomes available from an ever-growing collection of online sources, the value of research and information fluency continues to escalate. Without guidance in developing these skills, students will likely have great difficulty effectively leveraging sources and utilizing the data available to them. Thus, now more than ever, today's teachers must familiarize themselves with the most effective means of locating, sorting, and evaluating online sources of information in order to impart these vital skills to their students.

Critical Thinking, Problem Solving, and Decision-Making

In addition to the previously considered standards, the capacity to think critically, effectively solve problems, and judiciously make decisions ranks among the most imperative of the 21st century. As noted by ISTE (2007), students should be able to "use critical thinking skills to plan and conduct research, manage projects, solve problems, and make informed decisions using appropriate digital tools and resources."

More specifically, students must be capable of pinpointing and describing authentic problems and important questions for inquiry. Students should also be prepared to develop and implement strategies for completing projects and arriving at solutions. While problem solving, they must be able to incorporate a variety of processes and diverse viewpoints as they consider alternative solutions.

The benefits of guiding students in developing such critical thinking, problem-solving, and decision-making skills cannot be overemphasized. In today's world, technological tools and resources, when implemented effectively, play a tremendous role in facilitating the expansion of these standards. In fact, increasingly more professional fields will demand that their incoming employees be proficient at exercising such skills through technological applications.

Students eagerly await opportunities to make use of technology in their quest to reason, solve problems, and formulate decisions. Away from school, many students spend much of their time doing so through digital games and online programs designed to challenge the mind and expand thinking processes. Yet when such opportunities for learning with technology are not available within classroom settings, students naturally find it more difficult to remain engaged throughout the school day.

There seems to be a chasm between how they are expected to learn at school, how they choose to engage their minds away from school, and what they will be expected to do once they enter the professional arena. But what if teachers were proficient in effectively implementing instructional technology within their lessons? How might such a shift serve to create new connections between classroom endeavors, the interests and passions students pursue on their own time, and the skills and abilities they will need to operate successfully in the future?

Digital Citizenship

Among their inventory of vital standards for 21st-century learners, ISTE (2007) also includes digital citizenship, or the ability to "understand human, cultural, and societal issues related to technology and practice legal and ethical behavior." Skills associated with digital citizenship include encouraging and making use of information and technology in a safe, legal, and responsible way. Additionally, students are expected to demonstrate constructive approaches to using technology, thus supporting collaboration, learning, and productivity.

Ideally, students should also exhibit a personal desire for lifelong learning and the initiative to support others in becoming responsible digital citizens. As students' access to technology continues to skyrocket at younger and younger ages, the importance of teaching them to safely and responsibly make use of such resources escalates as well. Students must ultimately decide whether to use their technological skills to benefit their lives and the lives of others or to squander this potential in place of lesser pursuits.

Those responsible for leading younger generations—including teachers—hold the potential to play a tremendous role in building excellent digital citizens of the future. But unless today's educators are equipped with the knowledge and practical experience of demonstrating digital citizenship in their personal and professional lives, how can they impart these skills to others? To what extent might guidance from a well-versed colleague assist in this endeavor?

Technology Operations and Concepts

ISTE's (2007) concluding and all-encompassing final standard states that students should "demonstrate a sound understanding of technology concepts, systems, and operations." This includes learners' knowledge and application of technological systems as well as the ability to select and utilize applications effectively and productively. Students of the 21st century should be able to troubleshoot systems and applications and to transfer their current knowledge in familiarizing themselves with new technologies.

As technical knowledge and skills become increasingly sought after in professional environments, neglecting to prepare students for this reality ultimately works to disservice them. The thought of squelching a student's potential to succeed later in life pains the heart of any impassioned educator. Yet by avoiding opportunities to implement instructional technology—whether due to lack of time, frustration, or fear of the unknown—students will have gaps in their schooling experience. These teachers inadvertently pass over opportunities to prepare their students for the road that lies ahead.

No dedicated educator would deliberately forgo the prospect of creating motivating learning experiences, just as no devoted teacher supports the idea of leaving students unprepared for the future. For those who desire more for their students, collegial coaching for technology integration holds the potential to grow educators' abilities to tap into the potential of instructional technology like never before.

RECOGNIZING THE BEST CANDIDATES TO COACH

In light of the undeniable magnitude of equipping teachers with the tools necessary to foster 21st-century learning experiences for their students, an important initial step involves selecting the teachers with whom to begin the coaching process. The most effective way to involve educators in collegial coaching is through individualized meetings with them. As noted by Charles Bishop Jr. (2001), "the path to organization change is through individual change" (4), and "change happens one person at a time" (1).

There exist numerous ways in which to engage teachers in coaching process for technology integration, and latter parts of this book will delve more specifically into those methods. No matter the strategies chosen to establish faculty buy-in, Knight (2007) notes that "what matters is that a) coaches start by listening and respecting teachers with whom they are interacting, and b) they communicate—more than anything else—that they are another teacher willing to help" (22).

In light of these imperatives, the following foundational questions arise: How should schools begin selecting candidates for coaching? Who would most benefit from participating in the coaching process? It seems intuitive to devote much time to considering the characteristics of quality coaches, and chapter 4 is devoted to this focus.

Yet schools must also give careful thought to the attributes of a fitting candidate for coaching. Clearly, potential coachees should demonstrate a desire to develop their professional skills and practices in regards to instructional technology integration. The attitude and outlook of candidates also requires conscientious thought. Maintaining a mind-set open to the possibilities of collegial coaching involves first trusting in the value of such a relationship. Unless a teacher personally cultivates a willingness to learn, or a teachable spirit, the likelihood of seeing benefits from the experience declines significantly.

As part of the process graduate students undergo while identifying potential teachers to coach, each engages in a conversation with their building administrator. In 2009, one of the participating coaches happened to serve as a teacher at a prestigious private school in the area. As the graduate student met with her school administrator to discuss which faculty members to select for the coaching assignment, this particular administrator volunteered herself to be coached.

This offer seemed a surprising and perhaps risky endeavor. Yet the administrator recognized her own need for guidance in integrating technology, and if she expected her faculty to do the same, she felt the need to become more proficient. She was willing to face areas of potential growth in her attempt to develop both personally and professionally. Although at the top of her "professional game," the administrator acknowledged her need for coaching and welcomed the challenge to implement unfamiliar tools and pedagogy firsthand.

She appreciated the significance of this experience in helping her to lead the school in being the very best it could be. This experience not only shaped the administrator's practice, but it also shaped her vision for technology integration on her own campus. Since this initial experience, she has hired two curriculum specialists with technological expertise who teach students during half of each school day and coach teachers throughout the remainder of their time.

Ultimately, this administrator witnessed firsthand the need for both content and technical expertise. To this day, her campus maintains a competitive edge within a competitive city, in part because of her willingness to acknowledge her own educational areas of growth and seek out individualized help. In the end, she transformed her weakness into a school-wide strength.

As noted by Gross (2006), "merely going through the motions of the [coaching] program will be a waste of time" (28). Gross proposes that in determining the fit of candidates for coaching, schools should ask such questions as, "Does this person approach his or her professional life in a way that values opportunities such as research-based mentoring?" (28). Furthermore, school leaders should seek out individuals "whose confidence is so authentic that they are comfortable making mistakes and anxious to learn from them" (28).

Furthermore, specifically in relation to coaching for technology integration, the most ideal candidates for coaching embrace their roles as educators of 21st-century learners. While recognizing their need for growth in areas of technological proficiency, they desire to more effectively incorporate technology into their classroom learning environments. Such teachers acknowledge the shifting tides within educational settings and aspire to take the necessary steps in meeting the changing needs of today's learners.

In the words of Anna, a graduate student coach at an elementary school campus,

> The ideal candidate for a coachee is an individual who is willing to be honest about their needs and open to the new solutions. They are not required to have a large amount of preexisting knowledge about technology but must be ready to learn. A good coachee is also interested in evaluating and revising lessons. They want to perfect their art of teaching, while accepting the fact it will always be a work in progress. A good coachee must demonstrate persistence; technology rarely works flawlessly every time. They must be willing to try again.

When seeking to identify potential coachees, out-of-the-box thinking and creativity play key roles in the process. Even colleagues who do not teach within core content areas might benefit from the assistance of a technology integration coach. Administrators (as in the previous example), administrative assistants, and specialists throughout the school community may be prime candidates for coaching.

One coach engaged in this type of out-of-the-box thinking as she endeavored to coach a reading specialist, a speech therapist, and a librarian at the public elementary school in which she teaches. Her planning with these colleagues led to, among other things, the invention of a new Spanish app, the development of teacher-created videos using an online screencasting tool, and the inauguration of the school's first Tech-a-Palooza, a daylong technology event at the conclusion of the year.

The next chapter outlines a proven model for effective collegial coaching for technology integration. In today's age of rapid digital expansion within educational settings and beyond, meaningful faculty development targeting technology integration is needed now more than ever. Collegial coaching offers hope to seasoned teachers desiring to provide their students with 21st-century learning experiences.

ESSENTIAL IDEAS TO REMEMBER

Currently, teachers face many new impasses not previously encountered by professionals in the field of education. Confronted with ever-increasing demands for accountability, many digital immigrants leading today's class-rooms constantly struggle to allocate time within their packed schedules to research cutting-edge instructional technology, let alone identify the means by which to integrate it into the required curriculum. Encouragement and assistance in doing so is needed now more than ever before.

Occasions to inspire and spark meaningful change through collegial coaching exist within schools everywhere. Classrooms abound with seasoned educators who are passionate about meeting their learners' needs through applicable, engaging, and student-centered lessons. Such teachers strongly desire to effectively incorporate instructional technology within their curriculum. The issue is not that these educators lack the "want to." Rather, they often lack the "how to." This is where the benefits of technology-centered collegial coaching come into play.

REFERENCES

Bishop Jr., C. H. *Making Change Happen One Person at a Time: Assessing Your Change Capacity within Your Organization*. New York: AMACOM, 2001.

Ertmer, P. A. "Teacher Pedagogical Beliefs: The Final Frontier in Our Quest for Technology Integration?" *Educational Technology Research and Development* 53(4) (2005): 25–39.

Ertmer, P. A., D. Conklin, J. Lewandowski, E. Osika, M. Selo, and E. Wignall. "Increasing Preservice Teachers' Capacity for Technology Integration through the Use of Electronic Models," *Teacher Education Quarterly* (2003): 95–112.

Gross, S. J. *Leadership Mentoring Maintaining School Improvement in Turbulent Times*. Lanham, MD: Rowman and Littlefield Education, 2006.

International Society for Technology in Education. *Standards•S*. (2007): Retrieved from www.iste.org/docs/pdfs/20-14_ISTE_Standards-S_PDF.pdf.

Knight, J. *Instructional Coaching: A Partnership Approach to Improving Instruction*. Thousand Oaks, CA: Corwin Press, 2007.

Purcell, K., A. Heaps, J. Buchanan, and L. Friedrich. "How Teachers Are Using Technology at Home and in Their Classrooms," In Pew Research Center. (2013): Retrieved from www.pewinternet.org/2013/02/28/how-teachers-are-using-technology-at-home-and-in-their-classrooms/.

Webster-Smith, A., S. Albritton, and P. Kohler-Evans. *Meaningful Conversations: The Way to Comprehensive and Transformative School Improvement*. Lanham, MD: Rowman and Littlefield Education, 2012.

Chapter Four

Applying the Basics of Coaching

Wouldn't it be amazing if we spent as much energy investing in experiences as we do investing in things?

—Ruzwana Bashir, CEO, Peek.com

Within this modern, digitally propelled pace of life, a plethora of new dilemmas consistently bombards the digital immigrants guiding today's classrooms. In addition to the ever-pressing directives for accountability—including high-stakes testing, more rigorous policies, and intensified curricular benchmarks—many educators simply lack the time and energy needed to explore the latest instructional technology. Furthermore, the thought of formulating applicable methods of integrating such resources into the required curriculum seems entirely out of the question.

Encouragement and guidance in incorporating instructional technology comprises a pressing need in modern educational settings. In light of the compelling assortment of evidence in support of the importance of and demand for effective technology integration, school leaders—including administrators, curriculum coordinators, and seasoned educators—need a proven model for effective coaching for technology integration.

The methods presented within this chapter have been employed in school settings for the past several years with great success, providing novice users of technology with enhanced confidence in utilizing technological tools in their own planning and teaching. In essence, these techniques offer a straightforward, clear-cut outline for those desiring to enrich the effectiveness and quality of technology integration within the environments in which they serve.

This chapter presents the specific elements of this map as well as ideas for how it might be applied to various school settings. Together, the steps of this model compose a cyclical structure in which coaches and coached teachers naturally progress between phases, only to commence the process again with new candidates. This model also serves as a means of assisting educational organizations in developing fresh coaches from previously coached teachers, thus allowing the cycle to transpire into a self-perpetuating process.

The following sections contain an overview of the collegial coaching model for technology integration, which comprises the basis for the remainder of the book. Readers will discover that the model is specific enough to guide the leaders and educators within a school, department, or teaching team through their initial experience in collegial coaching. Yet the model is also open to adaptation and differentiation, depending upon the circumstances, available resources, structure of the program, and characteristics of the participants utilizing this process.

It goes without saying that a one-size-fits-all approach to collegial coaching for technology integration will almost certainly fail to adequately meet the needs of any one school setting. Thus, this model was designed with the intention of providing a basic road map to implementing a collegial coaching program among teachers that allows for flexibility and personalization.

The speed at which participants travel, as well as the detours and pit stops they take along the way, will almost certainly—and necessarily—vary from school to school and program to program. Most importantly, coaches and coached teachers should be provided the necessary time and encouragement to enjoy the journey, reflect upon their travels, and remember that oftentimes the process is more important than the product.

KEYSTONES OF THE COLLEGIAL COACHING PROCESS

Some of the central ideas for the collegial coaching process are rooted and grounded in what is known as adult learning theory, or andragogy, and project-based learning. First identified by Malcom Knowles in the 1970s, adult learning theory focuses on six assumptions that address how adults prefer to learn. These assumptions emphasize collaborative, problem-centered approaches that highlight equality between teachers and students. The six principles of adult learning theory include the following:

- Adults are internally motivated and self-directed.
- Adults bring life experiences and knowledge to learning experiences.
- Adults are goal oriented.
- Adults are relevancy oriented.
- Adults are practical.
- Adult learners like to be respected.

In this approach to coaching teachers for technology integration, adults will obviously be asked to learn something new. Quite often, the skills and concepts to be learned have been avoided over time, often because the learner perceives them either as impractical or too challenging. Yet as the description of the model unfolds throughout this chapter, the methods involved and reasons for its success should begin to seem more evident.

In addition to building the model on the principles of adult learning theory, the integration of project-based learning is also embedded. Project-based learning combines both cognitive and social constructivist theories from Piaget and Vygotsky by posing authentic problems to solve in a partnership approach through dialogue, group processing, and reflection.

Although teachers are often encouraged to embrace and integrate project-based learning with their students, educators themselves are rarely taught using these methodologies. The benefits of project-based learning include increased motivation, critical thinking, problem solving, and the ability to transfer knowledge and skills to novel situations. Coached teachers found that using technology often included a shift from teacher-centered to student-centered teaching. All of these benefits, among others, were reported by teachers involved in the authors' case studies of coaching for technology integration.

A REAL-LIFE SOLUTION TO A REAL-LIFE PROBLEM

The model outlined within this chapter was birthed from an amalgamation of real-life classroom experiences, originating within the university at which the authors teach. As a component of a class project focusing on coaching for technology integration, graduate students with technology expertise were each required to coach three teachers on their respective school campuses.

In doing so, they sought to identify three unique projects to complete with each coached teacher, and the projects ranged from personal productivity to student-centered technology use. The coaches were required to invest at least fifteen hours with each teacher on their campus, but this time could include activities related to research, curriculum development, and consultation.

Within the past year, one of the coaches involved in the project—who also happens to be an instructional specialist—selected very strong educators who had previously avoided technology integration for myriad reasons. Pam, the coach, reported that she learned from these teachers that "people want to learn, and it is less threatening to work with someone else instead of in isolation." She also noted that these teachers finally felt free to "confess their areas of weakness so that those targeted areas could be addressed in a private setting with customized support."

As the model was gradually refined across several years, five steps have been identified as essential to the success of technology integration. As Pam remarked, "Coaching is nothing new to my district. We have been on the coaching bandwagon for many years, but this is the first time that coaching from the instructional technology perspective has been implemented."

Furthermore, she emphasized, "Now that we are on the verge of a technology implementation breakthrough, the timing of the internship was perfect! This type of professional development is more effective because it's not a one-shot, drive-by, 'wham-bam' done."

THE COLLEGIAL COACHING MODEL
FOR TECHNOLOGY INTEGRATION

As previously described, the collegial coaching model for technology integration is cyclical in nature, comprising phases that naturally intermesh with one another to form a complete, seamless whole. Although these steps are described in sequential order below, participants in the coaching process must remain mindful of the fact that coaches and coached teachers can—and even *should*—revert back to previous phases at any time throughout the process as necessary.

These steps are not meant as items to be "checked off" a to-do list upon "completion." In fact, due to the complex nature of human interaction within organizations and the various facets implicated, a cut-and-dry means of "checking off" any one step does not exist. Rather, participants' progress within phases and movements back and forth between them should be carefully reflected upon and repeated as the need presents itself.

Phase 1: Establish the Need

Before embarking upon any journey, those involved in the expedition should logically understand the need for or purpose behind their travels. Why must this journey take place? Are there professional reasons, personal reasons, or both? Will it be for the sake of adventure, learning and discovery, a break from habit, or some combination of those reasons?

Much like the act of planning a physical journey in life, successful programs within organizations should also find their basis in the genuine needs of constituents or participants. School leaders must first consult the potential audience, namely their teachers. If collegial coaching is to be a useful experience, it should be founded upon and designed to meet a definite need on the part of the educational setting and the potential participants.

However, it must be noted that a significant chasm can exist between what individual community members think they need and what they actually need, both in extent and nature of support. Additionally, it should be evident

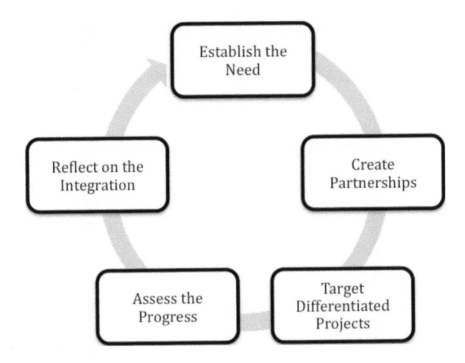

Figure 4.1.

that collegial coaching is the appropriate response to addressing issues of gaps in technology integration. In cases in which this has not been addressed, school leaders will likely encounter a group of teachers either uninterested in collegial coaching or possibly even resistant and unwilling to participate.

Before the coaching process is to begin, school leaders must seek to understand what those involved will want. If the coaching process will be initiated through a school committee composed of administrators, teachers, or both, it will be important to organize a thorough discussion establishing the time frame, involved participants and their roles, and other needed resources.

Alternatively, school leaders might implement plans to gather the teachers' input directly. Online surveys or questionnaires sent out via e-mail can serve as a time-effective, straightforward means of gathering information regarding individual teacher's needs, desires, and willingness to participate in the coaching process.

In considering the need for collegial coaching, school leaders must remain mindful of the fact that coaching is not only for those educators without experience or expertise in technology integration. It might also well serve veteran teachers who desire to fine-tune their knowledge and skills or would

Vignette: Establishing the Need

Creating a Faculty Needs Assessment

In order to understand the technology needs of her colleagues, Sue, an instructional technologist in an elementary setting, designed an online needs assessment survey. The survey was approved and sent out by her principal to faculty at the conclusion of the school year.

The survey included questions with open-ended responses. Teachers had the opportunity to share information regarding their most pressing needs for support, ranging from assistance with organizing digital files to designing more student-centered interactive whiteboard lessons to most effectively utilizing Web 2.0 tools.

That summer, Sue was able to review the data, research, and plan ways to address these needs through individualized coaching sessions, tailor-made for each colleague. This ultimately provided an excellent foundation on which to begin the new school year. Smart team!

Figure 4.2.

like to learn more about certain technological tools and resources they have not yet had the opportunity to explore or implement within their classrooms.

Before beginning the coaching process, school leaders must also decide whether participation will be voluntary or compulsorily assigned. Additionally, will participants be permitted to select their own coaching partners, or will partnerships be chosen for them? These crucial decisions will likely render a tremendous impact upon teachers' enthusiasm toward and interest in participating in the process.

Tips for establishing teacher buy-in are addressed more specifically in latter sections of this book. However, for the time being, it is important to remember that these initial decisions compose the crucial underpinnings of the program. These choices must be carefully and judiciously considered in order for the collegial coaching program to be built upon a firm foundation with unwavering, upward growth. It is also important that trust be established. Within the coaching setting, what is shared (strengths and weaknesses) must be kept confidential.

Just as importantly, those seeking to initiate a collegial coaching program must evaluate whether the leadership within the school stands united in wanting heightened technology integration. Is this a goal shared by only certain members of the administration and faculty, or is this something that every school leader earnestly desires?

School leaders must communicate why technology integration is important. Is it just a ploy to encourage the use of a variety of tools? Or is it a valuable endeavor focusing on the potential of technology integration to encourage a shift in pedagogy as well, with an emphasis on increased student engagement and achievement? They must determine if the school community is open to change and innovation, or if there are those among the administration and faculty that unreservedly (and even loudly) oppose such transformation.

In cases in which technology integration is not supported by administration, it might be best to initially focus upon finding ways to assist individual teachers in reaching their individual productivity goals, eventually gaining faculty buy-in as they see personal benefits. For example, is there a faculty member who would benefit from guidance and support in organizing the digital file system on his or her computer? Or might a certain teacher appreciate some assistance with sharing files with colleagues and parents via e-mail? These might be terrific candidates for coaching endeavors centered upon personal technological skills.

Once school leaders have the opportunity to witness how increased technological proficiency boosts certain teachers' confidence, enthusiasm, and personal productivity, those less inclined to the idea will likely have a change of heart. Additionally, when coaching partnerships focus on addressing predetermined outcomes together or seek to complete a certain number of technology-enhanced projects per semester, the coaching effort will gradually take on an increasing level of formality. As the support of school leaders grows over time, it can more easily be transitioned into an official collegial coaching program.

In the authors' case studies of collegial coaching for technology integration, once the teachers to be coached were identified, the coaches planned to individually meet with these teachers for an initial diagnostic interview. During these interviews, the coaches guided the teachers in exploring their fears, hesitations, insecurities, and overarching goals.

As previously mentioned, one requirement for the coaches in the program was supporting each of their three coached teachers through the process of implementing at least three new tools. Initial interviews served to assist the coaches and coached teachers in identifying areas of need and setting related goals. As one might imagine, when given the opportunity to self-identify and self-report areas to target, teachers were more personally motivated to see these projects to completion.

Coaches were allowed to work on campuses across the city with the support and approval of the building principals, and coached teachers were typically volunteers. At times, however, the principals identified individuals in need of additional assistance with technology integration, in order for the coaching program to boost their development in this area.

The opportunity to collaborate with a colleague ranked among the primary reasons the coaches and coached teachers attributed to the success of the program. In working collaboratively, they reinforced these aforementioned principles of adult learning theory:

- Adults are internally motivated and self-directed.
- Adults bring life experiences and knowledge to learning experiences.

In the words of past coaching participant Pam, it is highly important for the coach to "set the tone for the relationship." Additionally, there must be "respect, and the coach must listen to and understand the teacher's goals, ideas, worries, concerns, hopes, and dreams." Naturally, finding ways to build upon the coached teachers' strengths instead of focusing on weaknesses also leads to more positive and meaningful outcomes.

Phase 2: Create Partnerships

Within a collegial coaching program, the importance of thoughtfully and judiciously determining partnerships cannot be overemphasized. Among the most vital decisions in establishing a collegial coaching program, effectively matching coaches and coached teachers requires careful planning and consideration.

The formula for a successful strategic partnership may appear simple and straightforward: $1 + 1 = 3$. Indeed, partnerships often represent a viable means of enhancing the success of an organization, especially when they are rooted in effectual communication and collaboration. However, constructing productive groupings is not always as easy as one might assume.

Partnerships gone sour can lead to frustration, resentment, and a tremendous loss of time and community morale. A frequently referenced quote from the movie *The Godfather* is Don Corleone's mantra, "It's business, not personal." Yet this notion does not often hold true in partnerships, even in the professional settings of school environments. Because various characteristics

Vignette: Establishing the Need

Teacher-Centered to Student-Centered

Gabrielle is a high school AP Psychology and Spanish I and II teacher. On a scale of 1–5, he scored himself a 4 on technology use. He needed ideas for technology that gave students the power to use the tools.

His coach initially suggested using the Web 2.0 tool Quizlet since both disciplines are vocabulary rich. He (along with the coach) developed vocabulary lessons that provided practice and required them to complete online assessments. It also provided students vocabulary competitions that they really enjoyed.

The coach also introduced the teacher to another Web 2.0 tool called Glogster, where AP Psychology students created online presentations on abnormal psychology. Students included videos of their friends and family violating social norms. Very effective!

Figure 4.3.

and personalities will be at play in the coaching process, partnerships will undoubtedly encompass both professional and personal realms.

Thus, as partnerships are established, careful thought must be given to the willingness and abilities of coaches and coached teachers to communicate and collaborate with one another. When dealing with human relationships, one cannot guarantee and should not expect that the situation will remain free of conflict, no matter how cautiously matched the pairs. Most important is each partner's preparedness to effectively deal with and learn from conflicts when they do arise. Pairings along content areas or grade levels may serve to give both colleagues a common language as they begin the goal-setting process.

Vignette: Creating Partnerships

Coach Coworkers and Focus on Needs

Katherine and her coach, Tammy, were close colleagues for years; they even wrote curriculum together. Katherine rated herself as a 1 on a scale from 1–5 on technology use.

As the coach observed her classroom, she immediately realized that for any student-centered technology to occur, classroom management needed to be improved. She introduced her to the Web 2.0 tool Class Dojo. Adding this tool to her ActivInspire repertoire was an easy teacher-centered integration piece and allowed for additional student-centered integration moving forward.

Katherine and Tammy worked together later to integrate stop-motion videos using a familiar tool, PowerPoint. Students loved creating these videos. Next they plan to create online student portfolios using Weebly.com. These tools all work together to make Katherine's integration projects a great success.

Figure 4.4.

Ultimately, the coach and the coached teacher should work as partners. It is best if the coach refrains from dictating and instead listens as the coached teacher expresses his or her needs. Each partner must maintain a willingness to collaborate and a flexible attitude as they plan the integration pieces together. Partnerships should remain focused upon the concepts to be taught through identifying and following an action plan for achieving set goals.

Obviously, mutual respect comprises a vital aspect of successful coaching relationships. When peers coach peers, participants will sometimes find it easier to communicate with a colleague than they might with a superior. In addition, when coaches and coached teachers discover that they face similar issues in their professional worlds, supportive social and professional net-

Vignette: Creating Partnerships

Working Together to Reach Common Goals

During their second year of teaching first grade together, Jess, Adam, and Belinda decided to incorporate technology in their author biography unit. With their school's recent purchase of an iPad cart, the team decided it was a perfect time to update the unit.

Jess, an instructional technology graduate student, offered to coach her colleagues in implementing several new Web 2.0 tools she had discovered in her courses. The team collaborated to select the tools they wanted their students to use—including Little Bird Tales and Tagxedo—in presenting their learning about various authors.

Jess first "piloted" the tools with her students, allowing her to offer feedback and support to her colleagues. By sharing her experiences with her teammates, Jess helped Adam and Belinda to feel more confident about integrating new technology with their own students. They are eager for their next round of technology implementation.

Figure 4.5.

works often naturally transpire. In collegial coaching, a vital component of the reflective process includes self-identification of personal and professional goals that are consistent with one's values (Bland, Taylor, Shollen, Weber-Main, and Mulcahy 2009).

Aside from personality considerations, the creation of partnerships also involves more technical concerns. In some situations, it is best that a coach be paired with someone who teaches similar content areas, thus increasing the likelihood that he or she will be able to support and guide the coached teacher through curriculum-specific projects.

In elementary school, content-similar pairings are typically not difficult, as many primary educators teach multiple, if not all, subject areas. In such cases, pairs might be chosen within grade-level teams, in order for coaches to assist with endeavors spanning various content areas within one grade level.

However, in secondary environments, the subject area will sometimes determine the appropriate technological tools. In higher-level settings, applicable technology may differ vastly between content areas, depending upon specific learning goals or projects. For example, fitting technological tools and resources within a high school calculus classroom will likely be very different from those appropriate in an American history or English classroom.

Additionally, Fibkins (2011) suggests that administrators play an active role in the coaching process. They might even form a mentoring team made up of principals, assistant principals, department chairs, curriculum coordinators, and/or teacher leaders. Administrators can train these mentors regarding goals, objectives, and other foundational aspects of the program. In time, these individuals will then be able to train others within the school community to be mentors. Such teams might meet periodically to support each other in the coaching process.

In the authors' case studies of collegial coaching, the initial interview provided the coaches with insights regarding the content to be addressed within the coached teachers' curricular guidelines. These understandings provided a foundation from which the partners then brainstormed for methods and tools to utilize in teaching or assessing content. Former coach Lindsay found that when she met with her coached teachers, "We started with what they did in the past, and then talked about how we could tweak their already great lesson or unit to include technology to either deliver content or allow students to demonstrate their learning."

Fellow coach Pam remarked, "It was important to frame our conversations with, 'We are learning together!'" In an article published in *Educational Learning*, Knight (2011) described the tremendous value in reciprocity. He defines reciprocity as the belief that each learning interaction is an opportunity for everyone to learn. In other words, "When one teaches, two learn."

As previously described, once coached teachers are more fully trained and have been given time and opportunity to develop confidence and skill in technology integration and the coaching process itself, the coaching circle can widen. These coached teachers will soon be able to coach others, thus perpetuating the cycle. Eventually, this will hopefully lead to a school-wide coaching process in which all members of the school community have the opportunity to be a leader and a learner.

Phase 3: Target Differentiated Technology Projects

Once partnerships have been formed, coaches and coached teachers should be ready to begin focusing their attention on addressing the goals or projects established in their initial interview. This phase directly relates to the following principles of adult learning theory:

- Adults are goal oriented.
- Adults are relevancy oriented.
- Adults are practical.

Because adults learn best in situations through which they have the opportunity to address a set goal or goals, well-defined projects should be determined early within the coaching process. In doing so, the coaches and coached teachers will be able to more readily progress with focus toward a set target, rather than risking wasted time and flagging motivation by proceeding aimlessly into the unknown.

Additionally, adults prefer to work toward goals that seem relevant to their personal and professional needs. Thus, the targeted projects should be highly applicable to their objectives for themselves and their students.

Finally, because adults learn best in situations they perceive as practical, goals for achieving set projects must be reasonable. Before embarking upon any projects, coaches and coached teachers should consider such questions as the following:

- Can this project be completed within a reasonable amount of time?
- If not, can this project be divided into smaller, more manageable components?
- Once completed, can this project realistically be incorporated into the coached teacher's professional activities?

When beginning the coaching process with a teacher inexperienced in technology integration, coaches should first focus on goals related to personal productivity. For example, the coach should consider what types of teacher-centered technology use might assist his or her coachee in streamlining daily activities, such as e-mail use, digital file organization, presentation creation, and other such efforts.

As an initial integration piece, coaches should seek to focus upon a project that can be accomplished somewhat easily and within a relatively short amount of time. This will assist coached teachers in quickly realizing the benefits of technology integration, and it will most likely provide them with a boost of confidence and increased motivation to take on more challenging projects.

Once coached teachers have achieved small successes in incorporating technology for heightened personal productivity, coaches can play an integral role in helping them transition from teacher-centered to student-centered technology use. When deciding upon new projects to pursue, coaches and

Vignette: Differentiated Projects

Coaching across Different Content Areas

Jaime, a fairly new teacher, is a dance instructor in the high school. She rated herself a 4 on a scale of 1–5 on technology use. She later confessed that all of her experience is personal technology use, not using it in the classroom.

Her coach, Julie, was a social studies teacher with little expertise in the discipline of dance. After much dialogue, the two partners decided the best application for student technology use was aiding students as they collected and edited free online music for a dance routine.

Students were initially exposed to Web 2.0 tools like Classical Cat, Seekasong, and Jamendo. Eventually they used SoundCloud for editing music. As Jamie and Julie researched how to use the tools, Jaime was also coached in how to create a screencast with directions for how to use the tool. The coach got a double integration bang for her buck!

Figure 4.6.

coached teachers must remember this simple yet vital motto: "Content is king!" Before determining the tool or methodology to be employed, teachers should first focus on the content to be addressed. This will provide greater purpose and meaning behind the integration process, and it will also result in a more relevant and applicable final product.

As coaches are seeking to assist their coached teachers in implementing a new technology resource or tool, they should utilize modeling whenever possible. Much research has demonstrated that modeling is an effective instructional strategy in that it allows learners to examine a teacher's thought processes. By utilizing this form of instruction, educators are able to engage students in the imitation of certain behaviors that incite authentic learning.

Vignette: Differentiated Projects

Coaching across Different Content Areas

Robert, a fourth grade humanities teacher, loves to use technology as he teaches. When his students began to comment that they would like to use these tools in other classes, Robert felt led to address their request.

At the next fourth grade team meeting, he shared his successes, and several teammates in other content areas expressed interest in using some of the tools Robert had used.

After establishing curriculum needs, Robert suggested using Padlet, a Web 2.0 tool, as a means of providing developmentally appropriate, safe Internet resources as they research, collaborate, and communicate their learning.

They all found that Padlet was a terrific student-centered tool they used across several disciplines. Integration was a success, and the other teachers were soon ready for more technology tool ideas.

Figure 4.7.

According to social learning theorist Albert Bandura (1977),

Learning would be exceedingly laborious, not to mention hazardous, if people had to rely solely on the effects of their own actions to inform them what to do. Fortunately, most human behavior is learned observationally through modeling: from observing others one forms an idea of how new behaviors are performed, and on later occasions this coded information serves as a guide for action. (2)

Every day, countless teachers effectively incorporate modeling to enhance student learning across disciplines and throughout a variety of grade levels.

In this same way, coaches can also use modeling to assist colleagues in successfully integrating instructional technology within their own classroom learning environments.

In the aforementioned collegial coaching case studies for technology integration, the power of project-based learning surfaced as a pervasive, fundamental theme. Over the course of one particular semester, fifteen graduate students who were also teachers coached forty-eight colleagues across the city on fifteen different campuses. These coaches exposed the coached teachers to fifty-four distinct technology tools.

As one might imagine, in certain instances, after a coach had met with a teacher and established the content to address, the pair still felt uncertain about the most effective technological resources to implement with students. In such cases, two things took place. First, the coach had to candidly explain to the partner that he or she was unsure of the best course of action. Secondly, coaches in this situation would offer to conduct further research and report back to their partner with potential solutions.

This set of circumstances seemed to reinforce the idea that both the coach and the coached teacher were learning together. It also indicated to the coached teacher that integrating technology is not always easy. In fact, it cannot often be accomplished without time, energy, and careful thought invested both in and out of the classroom.

In some cases—particularly when a coach was paired with a colleague outside of his or her content area expertise—even extensive research did not provide the answers needed to address the issue at hand. At these times, the coach was encouraged to reach out to other coaches within the graduate class setting to help with brainstorming effective technology tools to apply. If an administrator had a team of coaches on his or her campus, then brainstorming with other coaches could take place in this setting.

This collaborative brainstorming approach ensured that no one was left on his or her own to solve integration problems. Thus, everyone involved in the process was provided someone to rely upon for collaborative assistance or support in thinking through various ideas.

Phase 4: Assess the Progress

Assessment represents a vital component of any collegial coaching program, primarily because it helps coaches and coached teachers determine whether or not the goals of the coaching process are being met. More specifically, it enables them to determine whether improvement in both technology integration and student-centered pedagogy are taking place. Assessment influences decisions about coaching needs and the direction that future coaching endeavors should take. It also inspires coaches to ask these essential questions:

- Am I teaching what I intended to teach?
- Is my coachee achieving the goals and completing the projects upon which we agreed to focus?
- Is there a better way to teach this concept, thereby promoting higher achievement and involvement by students or more effective integration of technology?

Coaches and coached teachers must carefully consider the process of learning new concepts or skills—not only by the coached teacher but also by his or her students. Also, they must evaluate which partners did what, taking into account each coached teacher's level of dependence upon the coach through each project. Ideally, the coachee should grow less and less dependent upon the coach over time, in direct relation to his or her developing abilities and confidence levels.

When applied to the collegial coaching process, assessment might assume a variety of meanings. It can be both formative and summative, and assessment can also be conducted either informally or formally. It is important that assessment take place at each meeting—during the planning process, throughout the integration process, and at the conclusion of every project.

In fact, each time a coach and coached teacher meet, both partners should assess the process and the product. The coach is responsible for assessing the needs of the teacher and offering options for integration tools and methods. Simultaneously, the coached teacher should assess the options presented, attempting to determine the best solution to address the needs of his or her students.

When formative assessment occurs in the planning process, both the coach and the coached teacher ought to assess the available resources and potential implementation schedules. In addition, the coach and the teacher might construct rubrics with which to assess student products. Once the implementation occurs, the assessment transforms from formative to summative. These summative assessments are primarily addressed in the subsequent stage, reflection.

Phase 5: Reflect on the Integration

As in any worthwhile endeavor, reflection is a crucial element for success within the collegial coaching process. Over the years, reflection has been consistently regarded as an indispensable teaching behavior by educational researchers (Dewey 1933; Langley and Senne 1997). Such reflection may be described as a dynamic engagement of the mind to disentangle problems (King 2008). Furthermore, reflection is thought to be a critical analysis involving self-awareness and heightened understanding (Dewey 1933). Ac-

Vignette: Assess the Progress

Using Assessment and Accountability to Generate Opportunities for New Ventures

Hannah, a technology coach, meets regularly with her administrator to discuss faculty progress on integrating technology. Successes are shared, and together they identify plans for addressing faculty hesitations and ideas for building increased faculty buy-in.

Both professionals demonstrate respect and empathy for their colleagues while addressing their progress. While it seems that Hannah is violating trust by reporting successes and failures to the administrator, faculty view it as an opportunity for reflection and celebration rather than condemnation. This, of course, has a lot to do with the way the administrator deals with information from the coach.

In this case, the administrator regularly celebrates successful technology integration implementations at each monthly faculty meetings and over time; these celebrations entice others to consider technology integration. A win for all!

Figure 4.8.

cording to Dewey (1933), reflection "converts action that is merely appetitive, blind, and impulsive into intelligent action" (17).

Reflective educators are not afraid to ponder "the good, the bad, and the ugly." They devote time and energy to thoughtfully considering questions such as the following:

- What parts of this experience went well?
- What did not happen as intended?
- What should be tried next?
- What changes need to be made to the situation?

Vignette: Reflection on Integration
Sharing Successes

Pam was a district specialist who coached another specialist. The coached teacher was very confident in his content but lacked technology expertise.

The teacher was coached on how to use Google Docs as a collaboration tool and Lino It! for student-created autobiographies with second graders, along with Quizlet and Socrative for the entire grade level for both formative and summative assessment purposes. Lino It! was on the district approved list, but students could not log into it. That needed to change before it was used again.

This educator felt so confident with each of the tools used that he began immediately sharing the tools with coworkers he met with across the district. They began to see immediate advantages in allowing students to produce products that showcase and demonstrate content knowledge in order to assess their learning.

Figure 4.9.

The coach and coached teacher should collaborate in reflecting upon and seeking answers to various questions regarding student learning, including:

- What did the students learn from this activity?
- Did they learn any more or less than they have in the past without technology integration?
- Was the best tool applied in this particular circumstance and setting?
- What should be adapted for next time?
- What was the best part about this integration piece?
- What was the most challenging element of this integration piece?
- How might this same tool/application be applied to another unit/lesson?

- Did the students demonstrate higher levels of thinking?
- Did the students achieve the levels of knowledge and comprehension required?
- Were there any changes in student motivation?

As a reminder, reflection and the preceding four phases represent a cyclical structure in which the steps can and should be reverted back to as necessary. Phases three, four, and five—targeting differentiated projects, assessing the progress, and reflecting on the integration—represent especially important opportunities for return visits.

Coaches and coached teachers should seek out new projects on which to focus; and in doing so, they must also remain mindful of the need to thoroughly assess the progress achieved at varying points throughout the process for both teachers and students. In addition, time and energy should be devoted to reflection on a regular basis, as this represents an essential component for meaningful and lasting change.

In revisiting these phases of the process, coaches and coached teachers set themselves up for achieving even further success. The more experience teachers gain in tackling new technology integration challenges, assessing their progress, and reflecting upon their efforts, the higher their confidence soars and the more their students ultimately benefit, both academically and technologically.

AN INVESTMENT WORTH MAKING

As the expression goes, "Give a man a fish, and you feed him for a day; show him how to catch fish, and you feed him for a lifetime." Much as this proverbial saying suggests, the process of learning a skill comprises infinitely greater worth than a one-off handout. This line of thought closely relates the process of guiding a teacher as he or she learns to effectively integrate technology. The infinite dividends yielded by this investment greatly outweigh the time and energy required to do so.

Nearly anyone with some sense of technological proficiency can recall a time when a family member, friend, or colleague required assistance in completing a task or solving a problem involving a technological difficulty. In such instances, there is often a tremendous temptation to provide a "quick fix" without taking the time to explain the thought process or steps to the solution. Yet one might reasonably assume that the very next time such an issue presents itself, the very same situation will likely occur again.

However, as time and effort are devoted to teaching the struggling individual how he or she can go about solving similar problems, so grows the likelihood of increasingly independent future problem-solving efforts. This

Vignette: Reflection on Integration

Leveraging Infectious Enthusiasm

Lydia, a recent graduate and new second grade teacher, felt very uneasy incorporating the "latest and greatest" technological tools in the classroom even though she was a digital native in her personal life. However, her student teaching tech exposure was limited to an overhead projector. Lydia felt entirely lost when it came to integrating technology.

She recognized her own weaknesses and sought assistance in integrating technology from a successful, experienced, technology-using teammate, Steven. Steven was a veteran teacher with thirty years of experience who regularly sought ways to integrate technology into his teaching. The two of them worked together for a semester, integrating technology and reworking curriculum.

Her enthusiasm for student-centered technology use spread rapidly, and she jumped at the chance to coach Rose the following school year.

Figure 4.10.

line of thinking effectively translates to the process of supporting and guiding teachers as they address real-life, personally meaningful technology integration challenges.

ESSENTIAL IDEAS TO REMEMBER

This chapter outlines a proven model for effective peer coaching for technology integration. These methods have been used for the last several years with great success, providing new technology users with confidence in their own teaching and planning.

When bolstered by a firm foundation of coaching, teachers' likelihood of being able to efficaciously tackle such issues on their own—with confidence and tenacity—increases dramatically. And once effectively coached teachers develop the assurance and skill to successfully incorporate instructional technology and address the associated challenges, they naturally become leaders within their teams and other spheres of influence. Soon, such educators grow into ideal candidates for coaching others within their school settings. And so the cycle continues.

REFERENCES

Bandura, A. *Social Learning Theory.* New York: General Learning Press, 1977.
Bland, C., A. L. Taylor, S. L. Shollen, A. M. Weber-Main, and P. A. Mulcahy. *Faculty Success through Mentoring: A Guide for Mentors, Mentees, and Leaders.* Lanham, MA: Rowman and Littlefield Education, 2009.
Dewey, J. *How We Think: A Restatement of the Relation of Reflective Thinking to the Educative Process.* Chicago: D.C. Heath, 1933.
Fibkins, W. L. *An Administrator's Guide to Teacher Mentoring.* Lanham, MA: Rowman and Littlefield Education, 2011.
King, S. E. "Inspiring Critical Reflection in Preservice Teachers," *Physical Educator* 65(1) (2008): 21–29.
Knight, J. "What Good Coaches Do," *Educational Learning* 69(2) (2011): 18–22.
Langley, D. J., and T. Senne. "Telling the Stories of Teaching: Reflective Writing for Preservice Teachers," *Journal of Physical Education, Recreation and Dance* 68(8) (1997): 56–60.

Chapter Five

Developing Quality Coaches

As we look ahead into the next century, leaders will be those who empower others.

—Bill Gates

Among his countless accomplishments, Aristotle is famously credited with the notion that "the whole is greater than the sum of its parts." The truth of this theory can be observed across a variety of situations and environments. For example, imagine a simple, austere clump of graphite—little more than a collection of carbon atoms. When placed under enormous pressure for a period of time, the graphite eventually produces a diamond, the most solid— and some would say striking—substance on the planet. This represents one of nature's finest illustrations of the whole being greater than the sum of its parts.

In some ways, developing quality coaches is similar to creating diamonds. The effectiveness and success of any collegial coaching program is highly dependent upon the quality of its components or resources. The attention to planning, amount of time allotted, available technological tools, support from administration, and many other elements all represent important components. The quality of the coaches, however, might just be the most vital of these elements. Without quality coaches, in fact, the possibility of a quality coaching program does not exist.

Much like making diamonds, the process of developing quality coaches seems straightforward in theory. However, it can be challenging in practice, and excellent coaches are rare and should be cherished and supported within their organizations.

In reality, no magical formula exists for acquiring outstanding coaches, and this chapter is not intended to provide readers with one. However, one thing can be known for certain. Developing a team of coaches greater than the sum of its parts is, to a certain degree, a function of the leadership involved in the coaching program. The following chapter offers a guide for school leaders as they seek to identify and grow excellent coaches from within their ranks.

This chapter also underscores the distinctive perspectives offered by many digital natives within the field of education. Collegial coaching allows digital natives and digital immigrants to collaborate through a professional helping relationship. The coach with technology integration experience and know-how supports the learning and acquisition of new technology skills by a colleague. This relationship represents a professional development vehicle by which educators can learn to integrate technology with success.

COACHES REPRESENT LEADERS OF CHANGE

In his book entitled *Leadership Mentoring*, Steven Gross (2006) explains that excellent mentors share certain unique characteristics. This chapter highlights some of these distinct qualities, discovered both through the authors' own coaching experiences as well as in research regarding collegial coaching and leadership. Within the authors' coaching case studies, graduate students nearing the conclusion of their collegial coaching experience were asked to share their thoughts regarding the characteristics of a quality coach.

In the words of Nathan, a coach on a private school campus, "The ideal coach needs to be well informed and knowledgeable in pedagogy and best practices. He or she must be willing and able to learn about other content areas and disciplines, and he or she should enjoy researching and exploring new ideas."

Furthermore, as Nathan explained, "A coach should be an experienced, excellent classroom teacher because he or she must apply ideas, concepts, strategies, and resources to a real classroom in a practical way. Coaches should also be optimistic and realistic, capable of developing a vision and setting goals for other teachers. Most importantly, the coach should practice humility and genuinely seek to meet the needs of the teacher."

Quality coaches, among many other things, are leaders of change. Research and practical wisdom support the notion that a great leader must first be an effective teacher (Tichy 2009). Fitting candidates for coaching cultivate a desire to learn new things and a willingness to devote the time and energy necessary for doing so. Additionally, they possess courage enough to participate in unfamiliar experiences.

They naturally yearn to step out of their own comfort zones, to employ out-of-the-box thinking, to challenge and stretch themselves, and to develop as people and professionals along the way. Furthermore, coaches find joy and excitement in the journey as they make inroads that lead others to experience new learning opportunities and processes of development.

Quality coaches view themselves as lifelong learners and cherish opportunities for discovery and growth. In doing so, they find ways to care for themselves and deflect negativity or other hindrances to development along the way. Such individuals conscientiously remind themselves that pushback from others is often not personal. Rather, those resistant to new experiences and change often feel this way due to their own fears and insecurities. Quality coaches "keep on keeping on" in spite of any obstacles that present themselves. They view every challenge as a fresh opportunity for growth and progress.

THE COMBINED FORCES OF
TECHNOLOGY AND TEACHING EXPERTISE

Effective coaches exhibit technology and teaching expertise (both teacher-centered and student-centered). Furthermore, their proficiency in each of these areas should be evident to colleagues within their school environments. When a teacher naturally and consistently demonstrates skill as an educator as well as the ability to effectively integrate technology, he or she will inherently hold greater credibility as a coach among peers.

In order to increase the expertise of coaches involved in collegial coaching case studies, the graduate student participants completed courses involving technology integration. In doing so, they were required to extensively incorporate technology within their own content areas using a variety of tools and techniques. Furthermore, these students were asked to plan for instruction assimilating multimedia, data manipulation software, Web 2.0 tools, Web authoring tools, brainstorming tools, and online collaboration tools for both teacher and student productivity.

Additionally, they were frequently exposed to presentations of fellow graduate students who integrated technology outside of their familiar content areas and grade levels. Watching these presentations helped the coaches to brainstorm uses for technology for a variety of age groups and content areas. Over time, the coaches compiled a database full of ideas for technology integration for a variety of settings.

HALLMARKS OF COACHING IN THE DIGITAL AGE

As technological advancements and applications continue to flourish within educational settings—not to mention every other aspect of life—coaches must position themselves to assist their fellow teachers in learning and applying the abilities and practices of professionals within the digital age. They should be prepared to encourage, support, and guide their colleagues to begin the shift toward welcoming and embracing the vast possibilities of instructional technology.

Effective coaches recognize that in this modern day and age, merely being able to use technology is no longer enough. Coaches of the 21st century must confidently and competently lead colleagues in applying technological tools and resources to explore alternative methods of delivering content to their students, determine novel ways to engage them, identify innovative methods for assessing student content knowledge, and discover new options for enhancing personal productivity.

ESSENTIAL CHARACTERISTICS OF COACHES IN THE DIGITAL AGE

The International Society for Technology in Education (ISTE) provides a set of six standards essential for coaches to effectively support and guide colleagues in preparing their students to thrive within an increasingly global and digital world. Visionary leadership ranks at the forefront of this list. More specifically, coaches of the 21st century "inspire and participate in the development and implementation of a shared vision for the comprehensive integration of technology to promote excellence and support transformational change throughout the instructional environment" (ISTE 2007).

Visionary Leadership

Coaches with visionary leadership assist their school communities in establishing, communicating, and executing a shared mission for the application of technology to reinforce meaningful learning experiences for every student. Furthermore, they contribute to the design, expansion, communication, execution, and assessment of technology-immersed strategic plans at the classroom and school-wide levels and beyond.

Through their actions, they promote the value of effective technology integration and support the realization of the shared vision embodied in their schools' strategic plans. Coaches who are visionary leaders also plan and execute novel approaches for instigating and maintaining technology innovations. They embrace and support the resultant change process that takes place within their school, thus setting an example by which others might be encouraged to do the same.

Teaching, Learning, and Assessments

As a vital component of their visionary leadership, quality coaches also guide their colleagues in teaching, learning, and assessment. According to the ISTE

(2007) guidelines for coaches of the digital age, successful technology coaches "assist teachers in using technology effectively for assessing student learning, differentiating instruction, and providing rigorous, relevant, and engaging learning experiences for all students."

In seeking to address these fundamental goals, excellent coaches do the following:

- Guide colleagues in and model the effective planning and implementation of technology-infused learning endeavors focusing on content and technology standards
- Guide colleagues in and model the effective planning and implementation of technology-infused learning endeavors utilizing a variety of student-centered instructional and assessment strategies founded upon educational research
- Guide colleagues in and model engagement of students in problem-solving endeavors that provide them the opportunity to investigate real-life issues, collaborate with others within their school and across the globe, and generate meaningful solutions
- Guide colleagues in and model the effective planning and implementation of technology-infused learning endeavors promoting creativity and critical thinking
- Guide colleagues in and model the effective planning and implementation of research-driven best practices in instructional design

Digital Age Learning Environments

Beyond coaching colleagues in effective practices regarding teaching, learning, and assessment, quality coaches also work to establish and maintain digital age learning environments within the schools at which they serve, thereby expanding the learning experiences of every student. For example, when working alongside colleagues, they model carefully planned and implemented classroom management and collaborative learning strategies. In doing so, they assist teachers and students in taking full advantage of the digital tools and resources at their disposal.

Furthermore, excellent coaches guide and support teachers in using Internet-based and hybrid learning platforms, digital content, and collaborative learning systems to reinforce and expand student learning. They also assist teachers in deciding upon, evaluating, and implementing adaptive and assistive technological tools and resources to enhance student learning. Moreover, they help in troubleshooting endeavors when software, hardware, or connectivity problems arise.

Professional Development and Program Evaluation

As previously mentioned, successful coaching programs begin with careful consideration of the needs of the involved faculty members. Furthermore, thoughtful and frequent assessment of how well the program is addressing these needs represents a vital component of the process. As explained in the ISTE (2007) standards, quality coaches "conduct needs assessments, develop technology-related professional learning programs, and evaluate the impact on instructional practice and student learning." Chapter 4, "Applying the Basics of Coaching," contains in-depth descriptions of these aspects of coaching.

Digital Citizenship

In this digital age, it is important to teach and model appropriate digital communication. Through the process of leading those within their school communities, quality coaches remain mindful of the importance of promoting digital citizenship. They support and model strategies for best practices related to appropriate technology use among teachers and students.

Excellent coaches demonstrate and promote safe, constructive, legal, and ethical approaches to making use of digital tools and resources. Moreover, they encourage cultural and global awareness through digitally based communication and collaboration tools, promoting appropriate and beneficial interactions with students, parents, peers, and others in the local community and beyond.

Content Knowledge and Professional Growth

Here again, the motto "Content is king!" holds true. Quality technology coaches consistently seek to develop and model professional knowledge and skills in content, pedagogy, and digital areas. Additionally, they must be able to apply theories of adult learning and leadership.

In order to do so, such coaches must be passionate about constantly expanding their knowledge and expertise. Because technology is ever-changing and always evolving, so too should be their learning endeavors. Excellent coaches are lifelong learners, continuously seeking to deepen their knowledge in effective technology integration. In doing so, they must consistently research, apply, and evaluate current and emerging technological tools and resources.

This continuous learning process should also serve to extend their knowledge and skills in organizational change and leadership as well as adult and project-based learning. Without question, quality coaches are reflective practitioners, frequently taking time to ponder and evaluate their professional practice, thereby devising and implementing strategies through which to adjust and improve their capacity to effectively model and facilitate technology-infused learning endeavors.

A SOLID REPUTATION: AS GOOD AS GOLD

As previously suggested, a reputation of proficiency in teaching and technology integration lends credibility to an individual's coaching endeavors. However, a coach's reputation must extend beyond his or her ability to effectively foster student learning and innovative technology integration. A successful coach must have a solid reputation, both professionally and personally. He or she must be well liked among colleagues, as this is foundational for establishing trust.

Excellent coaches possess not only strong content knowledge but also an "infectious personality," thus helping to encourage and inspire teachers to improve their practices (Steiner and Kowal 2007). Lindsay, a coach on a middle school campus, discovered that "coaches must be people with large servants' hearts, unafraid to lead or invest in another person."

Unless fellow teachers have confidence in the coaches responsible for guiding and supporting them, it is doubtful they will be willing to share needs and concerns about technology integration. Trust is an essential first step to inviting another individual into one's personal and professional spheres, especially when the process of learning an unfamiliar or challenging task is involved. It is often said that successful relationships are built upon trust, and this applies to coaching partnerships as well.

When trust has been established, the coached teacher is able to confess personal weaknesses to his or her coach with reassurance that this information will be openly shared among others. Only then can the weakness be addressed in a positive way, little by little. Through these one-on-one encounters, trust is reinforced, and slowly but surely, the coached teacher learns to lean and depend on the coach for technical support that extends past the classroom.

To establish this kind of trust, the coach must win the respect of his or her colleagues over time, through qualities such honesty, reliability, integrity, and a desire to go above and beyond. Coaches who are able to gain this kind of respect begin to carry a reputation. They are seen as individuals who put their professional reputation on the line each and every day, consistently seeking ways not merely to meet but rather to exceed expectations.

In regards to the significance of a good reputation, Socrates wisely advised,

> Regard your good name as the richest jewel you can possibly be possessed of—for credit is like fire; when once you have kindled it you may easily preserve it, but if you once extinguish it, you will find it an arduous task to

rekindle it again. The way to a good reputation is to endeavor to be what you desire to appear.

Because respect from one's colleagues is earned neither quickly nor easily, it is preferable that coaches be selected from within the campus on which they have been teaching for some time. Oftentimes, colleagues are more inclined to trust those with whom they have developed a solid working relationship.

When leaders are brought onto a campus from the outside world, confidence in their character and abilities may take longer to develop. However, in cases where this seems to be the only viable option, successful coaching programs are certainly still possible. Through dependably exhibiting venerable character traits such as those mentioned above, new coaches will gradually earn the trust and respect of their fellow educators.

THE POWER OF PRAISE

Quality coaches believe in the value of offering praise and celebrating success. The power of praise is that it reinforces the significance of a job well done and increases coached teachers' confidence and motivation to press on toward set goals. Teachers often have the opportunity to witness the vast potential of effectively shared praise as they interact with students in their own classroom learning environments. Many of the same principles used with students can also be successfully applied to coaching relationships.

Effective coaches actively shape their praise of coachees' progress in order to increase their motivational efforts. One way to do this is to specifically describe noteworthy gains in incorporating instructional technology. Praise such as "Well done!" is insufficient because it lacks description of specific progress or development (Hawkins and Heflin 2011). However, this statement becomes more meaningful when expanded to incorporate an explicit action taken, such as "You expertly used the new Web 2.0 tool we talked about to engage all of your students in that lesson today. Well done!"

Furthermore, excellent coaches find ways to commend their coachees' efforts and accomplishments, rather than focusing on their level of skill with technology integration. For example, a coach might mention, "The time and effort you've devoted to integrating this software program into your unit is really paying off. I can see how thrilled you are about your students' enthusiasm for this project."

On the other hand, coaches should avoid statements that focus on a teacher's ability—whether actual or perceived—to integrate technology. Remarks such as "I know it's really uncomfortable for you to think about how to include technology in this lesson, but I'm proud of you for trying" can ultimately discourage coached teachers. Instead, when commendation focuses upon a teacher's effort and achievements, it can serve to remind them of the direct relation between their diligence and the resultant development in effective technology integration.

Coaches must also be certain to let administrators in on their coached teachers' successes. Nearly everyone places great value in accomplishing something noteworthy in the eyes of their boss, and this is no exception. Most employees naturally relish and thrive on positive feedback from their superiors, using such acclamations as fuel for even greater dedication to growth.

However, as one might imagine, struggles or failures are best kept between the coach and coachee. Just as individuals flourish after a pat on the back from a supervisor, they often shrink back when their failures are brought out into the open before a boss. Discretion and other simple acts of thoughtfulness toward the coached teacher will achieve great gains in promoting a respectful and nonthreatening coaching environment.

Finally, coaches should help their coachees identify ways to promote student projects. In other words, partnerships must find ways to advertise the outstanding work their students achieve with technology. For example, the coach might support the coached teacher in using the school website to showcase students' digital products, open a faculty meeting with a brief show-and-tell, begin a parent meeting or open house with a "Did you know?" showcase, and the list goes on and on.

The confidence and excitement generated from thoughtful praise is contagious. Teachers naturally talk to one other, thus encouraging an incidental sharing of successes. Authentic celebrations of significant successes encourage ripple effects throughout a campus setting. As a teacher achieves personally meaningful goals or implements technology with triumph, he or she begins to feel more and more like an expert. These achievements are meant to be shared!

Effective coaches play an integral role in celebrating such triumphs. As they do so, they also remind their coached teachers of the value of sharing their new expertise with fellow colleagues, thus perpetuating the coaching cycle. Before long, those who were coached informally begin to share their successful student projects with colleagues, in effect coaching other teachers. This builds teacher confidence and, in turn, brings new opportunities for successful technology integration.

THE PERFECT LEADER?

This chapter describes a variety of characteristics and behaviors exhibited by excellent coaches. These qualities span a broad range of capabilities as well as personal and professional habits. And if any one coach were capable of consistently demonstrating each and every one of these various merits, he or she would certainly be "the perfect leader." Yet in considering these attributes, one must remember that in the real world, the perfect leader does not exist.

Within any situation or environment, a leader will unquestionably make mistakes. Additionally, every leader is only human and, as such, is on a path of development. No one will ever be capable of doing all things correctly at all times, and this cannot be expected. Furthermore, if a school community's idea of leadership is founded on the expectation of perfection, this faulty perspective will likely lead to frustration and disappointment.

The expectation of perfection in any environment is unwise, primarily because it cannot really be applied to any true form of leadership or coaching. Ultimately, the anticipation of perfection lacks fairness, common sense, and practicality. Although there is no such thing as the perfect coach, there is such a thing as a humble coach. Moreover, a coach's humility in the midst of imperfection might ultimately serve as the mark of a great leader. In reality, humility often offers a starting point for beneficial, creative, and lasting growth.

Humble leaders stand out in a society in which self-importance and "looking out for Number One" is often encouraged and even admired. In a "dog-eat-dog" world, humble leaders hold the amazing potential to effect positive change within their communities, including their school environments. People long for and are often refreshed by servant leaders who embody the rare trait of genuine humility.

By remaining open to criticism and not being afraid to make mistakes, humble leaders embrace opportunities for personal and professional development. In doing so, they also inspire growth in the lives of those around them. Just as quality coaches know how to celebrate success, they also see the value in accepting and learning from failure. They realize that the most worthwhile and meaningful successes are achieved in, through, and often because of past failures.

John C. Maxwell (2007), an internationally recognized leadership expert, speaker, coach, and author, offers these words of wisdom for leaders in any field, including collegial coaches: "Know that you're going to make mistakes. The fellow who never makes a mistake takes his orders from one who does. Wake up and realize this: Failure is simply a price we pay to achieve success." In many ways, the path to success in leadership can be found through embracing a simple yet profound motto: "Fail early, fail often, but always fail forward" (Maxwell 2007).

ESSENTIAL IDEAS TO REMEMBER

In regards to classroom technology use, digital natives, or teachers experienced with technology use, often possess valuable perspectives, knowledge, and skills that uniquely position them to profoundly impact the technology integration efforts of fellow educators. Collegial coaching provides a professional helping relationship and process in which a coach with expertise and experience aids the learning and acquisition of new 21st-century skills by a colleague. Such programs represent a professional development vehicle by which educators can learn to integrate technology with success.

Quality coaches are made—not born—as they humbly embrace, learn from, and develop through their own failures. The attributes of successful coaches are developed slowly and steadily over time. And each breakthrough along the way brings them one step closer to leaving a lasting impact upon the leaders, teachers, and students within their school communities for the better.

REFERENCES

Gross, S. J. *Leadership Mentoring: Maintaining School Improvement in Turbulent Times.* Lanham, MA: Rowman and Littlefield Education, 2006.

Hawkins, S. M., and L. J. Heflin. "Increasing Secondary Teachers' Behavior-Specific Praise Using a Video Self-Modeling and Visual Performance Feedback Intervention," *Journal of Positive Behavior Interventions* 13(2) (2011): 97–108.

International Society for Technology in Education. *Standards•C.* (2007): Retrieved from www.iste.org/docs/pdfs/20-14_ISTE_Standards-C_PDF.pdf.

Maxwell, J. C. *Failing Forward: Turning Mistakes into Stepping Stones for Success.* Nashville, TN: Thomas Nelson, 2007.

Steiner, L., and J. Kowal. *Instructional Coaching.* Washington, DC: Center for Comprehensive School Reform and Improvement, 2007.

Tichy, N. M. *The Cycle of Leadership.* New York: Harper Collins, 2009.

Chapter Six

Beginning on the Right Foot

You never really understand a person until you consider things from his point
of view . . . until you climb inside of his skin and walk around in it.

—Atticus Finch, *To Kill a Mockingbird*

Beginnings are crucial. The way in which new programs are presented within
a school community often sets the tone for the entire endeavor. Additionally,
participants' first impressions, initial feelings, and early feedback about the
program frequently generate a ripple effect, profoundly contributing to either
the success or eventual downfall of the undertaking.

Without doubt, educators appreciate the importance of first impressions
and the value of laying firm initial foundations—possibly better than anyone
else. Teachers spend countless hours planning the layout and design of their
classrooms, their curricular units and individual lesson plans, and their proce-
dures for ensuring a successful year—long before the tranquil days of summer are replaced by the buzz of student chatter on the first day of school.

Teachers understand the significance of well-laid plans. In fact, for many
educators, careful planning equates to success—and sometimes even survi-
val. Teachers realize that impressions can be long-lasting, and they are often
based upon only a quick moment of time or a thin slice of behavior. Before
they even begin teaching, their students will have already formed certain
impressions about them.

Much like the first day of school, the immense power of careful planning
and positive initial impressions can render a lasting impact upon efforts to
establish collegial coaching programs for technology integration. This chapter describes the process of constructing a firm foundation for a collaborative
learning environment in which teachers coach teachers.

RELATIONSHIPS MATTER

In learning, as in life, relationships matter. They matter because learning—whether by students or teachers—does not just naturally spring forth from ideas and plans. Learning does not take place on computer screens. Instead, genuine learning often originates through the interactions of people. And, as the oft-repeated saying goes, coached teachers, much like students, "will never care how much you know until they know how much you care." Therefore, the importance of relational foundations established in mutual trust, respect, and caring cannot be overemphasized.

Within collegial coaching case studies, this principle held true time and again. The value of devoting time, thought, and energy to growing quality relationships with coached teachers is clearly confirmed through the feedback of Anna, a technology integration coach on an elementary campus:

> The good relationship we previously established made it easier for me to understand their felt needs as teachers as well as departmental and school goals for technology use. Much of the technology used by my coachees had been introduced during faculty-wide professional development, but it was not until the technology was specifically adapted to fit their personal teaching style and lessons that it was implemented for classroom use. The close relationship I had with all of my coachees also encouraged additional accountability. The project ideas were more likely to be implemented because they valued my effort in assisting them and knew I would follow up. This relationship and the ability to individualize technology implementation are missing in most schools.

Anna also shared these words regarding the significance of a coach's efforts to be a strong relationship builder:

> The ideal candidate for serving as a coach is one who can build strong relationships with colleagues and establish trust based on their professional expertise. A coach must be flexible and able to adjust their goals to fit the perceived needs of their coachees. A coach must also be patient, realizing everyone is at different points in their development as a teacher. Finally, a coach must be able to problem-solve and find solutions to the needs of others.

In acknowledging the importance of solid relationships in the coaching process, the question of how to begin building such relationships naturally arises. Within the aforementioned collegial coaching case studies, the graduate student coaches devoted significant time to reading about and reflecting upon the basics of this practice as a component of their course requirements.

Resources they applied included *Using Technology with Classroom Instruction That Works* by Dean, Stone, Hubbell, and Pitler (2012); *Schools That Change: Evidence-Based Improvement and Effective Change Leader-*

ship by Lew Smith (2011); and *Understanding by Design* (2005) by McTighe and Wiggins (2005).

The coaches were also exposed to self-assessments to help them identify their strengths, dominant learning styles, and personality types. The principles advocated within these resources provided a foundation by which the coaches initiated interactions with their coachees, and key principles from these books are shared within this chapter.

FIRST KNOW THYSELF

Legend says that the ancient Greek philosophers, statesmen, and lawgivers responsible for establishing the groundwork of western culture once assembled in Delphi to engrave the words "Know thyself" at the doorway to its sacred oracle. Consequently, the saying morphed into a touchstone for Western philosophers and an often-quoted adage, even today. Plato is famously attributed the following take on this ubiquitous motto: "I must first know myself, as the Delphian inscription says; to be curious about that which is not my concern, while I am still in ignorance of my own self would be ridiculous."

In spite of the apparent importance of knowing oneself, this also represents a seemingly problematic—if not illusive—achievement. When asked to describe the most difficult task, the notable Greek philosopher Thales replied, "To know thyself." When asked to pinpoint the easiest, he replied, "To give advice." Admittedly, doling out suggestions to others often comes more naturally than devoting effort to thoughtfully reflecting upon one's own current state and opportunities for growth.

Regarding this subject, Benjamin Franklin advised, "Observe all men— thyself most." Would-be coaches begin building their own foundation for successful coaching experiences by learning more about themselves first, before seeking to guide others. Furthermore, effective coaches should also devote time to learning as much as possible about those they intend to coach.

In the initial coach training of the graduate case studies, the coaches were asked to learn more about themselves through completing several online learning style inventories. Additionally, it was suggested that they ask their coached teachers to do the same. The results of these inventories proved highly enlightening for coaches and coached teachers alike. Through reflection and identifying similarities and differences in learning styles, the coaches and coachees achieved great gains in determining strategies for working together effectively.

More specifically, these inventories indicated the intelligence type in which each of the participants felt most confident working to solve problems, based on Howard Garner's (1983) theory of multiple intelligences. Namely, they determined whether their dominant intelligence type fits into the linguistic (word smart), logical mathematical (numbers smart), interpersonal (people smart), intrapersonal (self smart), musical (music smart), bodily kinesthetic (body smart), visual spatial (visual smart), naturalistic (nature smart), or existential (spirit smart) category.

This particular online inventory utilized by coaches and coached teachers can be accessed via a number of online resources, including the following: www.bgfl.org/bgfl/custom/resources_ftp/client_ftp/ks3/ict/multiple_int/index.htm.

In addition to the multiple intelligences inventory, coaches also completed an online Myers-Briggs personality test. The Myers-Briggs Type Indicator personality inventory is designed to make the theory of psychological types proposed by C. G. Jung plausible and applicable to people's lives. In essence, Jung's theory explains that a great deal of the apparently random deviation in individuals' behavior is, in fact, fairly systematic and constant. In reality, these variations can be attributed to fundamental differences in the ways people choose to use their perception and judgment.

Although the coaches within the case studies did not complete the full version of the Myers-Briggs inventory, they did complete an abbreviated adaptation that allowed them to learn more about themselves and those they would be coaching. Through doing so, they were identified with attributes in four areas as either introverts or extraverts, intuitive or sensing, thinking or feeling, and judging or perceiving.

Basically, this inventory assisted the participants in discovering new insights regarding what gives them energy, how they take in information, how they make decisions, and even their day-to-day lifestyle preferences. The online test coaches used can be found at similarminds.com/jung.html. Furthermore, they gained enriched understandings of their strengths and weaknesses by reading through this supplemental site: www.16personalities.com/type-descriptions.

Finally, the coaches also completed a StrengthsQuest inventory, which assists users in identifying their top three strengths and one area of weakness. Additionally, the assessment provides participants with various action items for development and recommendations for making the most of their unique talents to accomplish heightened personal and professional success. The coaches completed an online version of this assessment, accessible via the following Web address: http://richardstep.com/richardstep-strengths-weaknesses-aptitude-test/.

ACHIEVING SOMETHING USEFUL THROUGH REFLECTION

Margaret Wheatley insightfully observed, "Without reflection, we go blindly on our way, creating more unintended consequences, and failing to achieve anything useful." Thus, reflection upon the results of the aforementioned inventories composed a vital foundation for the coaching process. In completing and reflecting upon these assessments, coaches were challenged to devote time to learning more about themselves. Through this process, they were compelled to examine and share significant information regarding their likes and dislikes, strengths and weaknesses, passions and struggles.

Furthermore, in contemplating their coachees' assessment results, the coaches achieved inroads toward learning more about those they were seeking to serve. Essentially, this process enabled them to listen to their coached teachers' perspectives and to reflect upon their understandings.

More specifically, the coaches were asked to reflect in the following ways:

According to the Myers-Briggs assessment, I am _____.

I see this as I work with other teachers especially when _____.

This means something I need to be careful of is _____.

This means I am especially good at _____.

According to the StrengthsQuest assessment, my top five strengths are _____.

This means something I need to be careful of is _____.

This means I am especially good at _____.

My top two learning styles are _____.

I see this as I work with other teachers especially when _____.

This means something I need to be careful of is _____.

This means I am especially good at _____.

This is what I learned about myself: _____.

This is how it affects my work with others: _____.

Through completing this process, many of the coaches conveyed inspiring and insightful "aha!" statements, including the following:

- I learned I am a "thinker" by nature and work through many problems or issues in my own head. I need to remember to help others see my own thought process and listen attentively to their thoughts and ideas.
- I am especially good at finding and doing what is best for students. However, this means I need to be careful of trying too much too soon.
- I need to be careful not to allow the tool or process to get in the way of the coach/coachee relationship and collaboration.
- I need to be careful to ensure that I am respecting and valuing the beliefs and ideas of my teachers, even when they differ from mine.
- I learned that I am a very determined person and that I need to have a purpose in my life and in my work. I believe this drive will benefit not only me but those around me as well. I just have to make sure I am always listening to the teachers I work with and that I am providing them with useful information and not overwhelming them with extraneous details they do not need.
- I need to understand and respect the teachers' thoughts, especially when they are voicing opinions that contradict what I believe is useful and worthy of implementation in the classroom.
- I must remember that not everyone is as interested or dedicated to technology integration as I am, and I cannot let that affect me personally.

UNDERSTANDING CHANGE
MANAGEMENT IN EDUCATIONAL SETTINGS

In Lew Smith's (2011) book *Schools That Change*, he highlights eight different schools that effectively managed change. These changes ranged from pedagogical shifts to physical enhancements to improved achievement levels for the students. This book helps those involved in changing paradigms to better understand the process of change and the characteristics of effective change leaders. Smith suggests that real change happens within a certain context, using positive conversations to help to build the capacity for change within each individual and school campus.

The updated version of *Using Technology with Classroom Instruction That Works* (2012), which was originally published by Marzano, has been utilized in coaching programs as well. This resource offers coaches ideas for technology integration tools specifically related to research-based strategies, proven to boost student achievement.

These strategies include setting objectives, offering feedback, providing recognition, cues, questions and advance organizers, nonlinguistic representation, summarizing and note taking, cooperative learning, and reinforcing effort. While technological innovation has greatly expanded since this book was first published in 2001, it still serves as an effective tool to spark ideas for new applications that address strategies to be shared, tried, and integrated.

The final resource coaches were asked to incorporate into their coaching is Wiggins and McTighe's (2005) *Understanding by Design*. This book grounds coaches in effective curriculum design strategies that are standards based, prompting educators to begin with the end in mind. Additionally, the book serves to focus teachers on creating assessments and essential questions students should be able to answer at the completion of every unit of instruction. With this emphasis, teachers and coaches are reminded to first prioritize content before thinking about tools or activities.

Establishing a firm foundation pedagogically with coaches and teachers is critical to achieving genuine innovation and advancement in teaching and learning. While focusing on reliable and research-based techniques is important, the relationship the coach and teacher spend time building is equally crucial. The above resources encompass important components to consider as school leaders determine the best strategies for beginning a coaching program within their school settings.

GREAT SUPPORT SYSTEMS LEAD TO GREAT COACHING

Behind every great coach is a great support system. Oftentimes within school settings, coaches serve as pioneers for innovation and meaningful change. Naturally, this unique role requires careful planning, steadfast confidence, and sometimes even an extra dose of courage.

Not only do coaches need support in brainstorming ideas for technology use, but they also need help with formulating strategies for working collaboratively and productively with other teachers. Generally, such support systems are best developed among a group of peers in which no one person holds any real (or even perceived) power over another. A collection of individuals that meets for the purposes of brainstorming can play a tremendous role in boosting coaches' creativity and confidence.

As remarked by Steven Covey, "When you really listen to another person from their point of view, and reflect back to them that understanding, it's like giving them emotional oxygen." Just as living organisms cannot survive—let alone thrive—without oxygen, coaching programs flourish best when participants are provided frequent opportunities for the sharing of "emotional oxygen."

Throughout the collegial coaching case studies, in addition to meeting individually with their teachers, the coaches also met every other week with one another. In these meetings, the coaches took turns introducing and explaining new and unfamiliar tools to the group. This way, the coaches were consistently exposed to innovative tools they might suggest to their teachers or use themselves. Furthermore, the sessions served as opportunities for the coaches to support one another professionally through collaborative brainstorming and sharing research on technology integration. These meetings were designed to facilitate growth for the coaches and assist them in dealing with real-world problems.

ORGANIZING INSTRUCTIONAL SUPPORT ENDEAVORS

Among a coach's most imperative responsibilities is supporting teachers as they seek to close the gap between what they know and what they are able to do. Instructional technology coaches assist their coachees not only in helping them learn new instructional technology tools but also new pedagogical approaches. Just as importantly, they guide colleagues in applying this newfound knowledge of instructional technology and pedagogy to their day-to-day classroom routines.

However, the continual expansion of technological innovations and methods of integration requires educators to navigate countless perspectives and recommendations for incorporating technology. An absence of coordination among myriad sources can lead to conflicting messages that serve to discourage hesitant teachers, possibly leading them to ultimately resist technology integration altogether.

Schools can effectively address this issue by seeking to ensure that all communications, tools, and strategies intended to support classroom technology integration are coherent and aligned. When this occurs, faculty members feel better prepared to clearly formulate goals with their coaches, to more easily develop plans for achieving those goals, and to more confidently and readily proceed in that direction.

FORGING ALLIANCES WITH ADMINISTRATION

Over time, the responsibilities of school administrators have gradually shifted away from management and operations and toward instructional leadership. However, few structures exist to assist them in successfully navigating these changes.

In fact, many school leaders still feel somewhat uncertain as to how to conduct an effective classroom observation. Countless others seem unsure of how to successfully guide their teachers in achieving meaningful growth as professionals, especially in the area of technology integration. The education system in general has yet to supply the resources, guidance, or support needed to assist in closing these crucial gaps in knowledge.

However, when administrators team up with coaches and lend their vital support to coaching programs, they hold the potential to achieve tremendous gains in tackling these issues. While upholding confidentiality with the coachees, coaches can reinforce the school leaders' perceptions of successful coaching methods to utilize with teachers struggling to incorporate instructional technology.

Furthermore, coaches also assist in developing action plans for relating the administrators' vision and priorities regarding technology integration to classroom environments. Working collaboratively, school leaders and coaches can explore and execute other activities that help the school expand and target teacher growth in instructional technology implementation.

When coaching programs flourish, schools communities are also more liable to form and develop a far-reaching vision for inspiring and supporting excellence in technology integration. Even more significantly, they better position themselves to cultivate environments of meaningful learning, effectively preparing to foster growth in the lives of teachers and students alike.

COACHING ACROSS GENERATIONS

Within this coaching model, relationships between coaches and coachees will often span generations—although not always—as digital native teachers (those experienced in using technology) seek to assist digital immigrant colleagues with technology integration. The cross-generational nature of these relationships might sometimes heighten differences in "outlook, worldview, work ethic, view of authority, leadership approach, and learning styles" (Bland, Taylor, Shollen, Weber-Main, and Mulcahy 2009, 117).

A recognition of possible variances in perspectives based upon age or generation often works to significantly further the success of coaching relationships. It is important to note that in such situations, however, stereotypes must be carefully avoided. As previously mentioned, mutual respect between both parties is vital. When coaches and coached teachers seek to acknowledge and appreciate diverse perspectives on teaching and learning, this often results in an even stronger relationship and richer coaching experience for both individuals.

As explained by Blank and colleagues (2009), generational characteristics render a tremendous impact upon how people see the world, make decisions, carry out their lives, and relate to others. It is important that partners in coaching relationships seek to understand each other's generational attributes, as this can assist them in grasping why people behave in certain ways, what they accept as true and hold dear, and how they tackle responsibilities at work and in life.

Obviously, it is often necessary to generalize when considering generational differences. Frequently, such generalizations can assist individuals in
gaining new understandings regarding another person. According to Raines
(2003), "They can give us the insights, awareness, and empathy that can lead
to new cohesiveness, creativity, and productivity" (11). Although all human
beings possess unique personality traits, they have also experienced various
events and circumstances in life that link them to their generation.

However, collaborative endeavors are enhanced when diverse generations
recognize not only their differences but also what unites them. Additionally,
generational qualities may vary among people of different cultures. Although
it is helpful to acknowledge the influence of generational affiliation on viewpoints and actions, it is also important to recognize that for varying reasons, a
person may or may not associate with particular attributes relating to his or
her generation.

Cross-generational coaching can serve as an instrumental and impactful
experience for coaches and coached teachers. Likenesses and differences
between generations often play a beneficial and enriching role in coaching
relationships. In the words of Martin and Tulgan (2002), members of varying
generations should "respect and honor [their] differences and approach them
not as a reason for conflict but as springboards to learning, productivity, and
innovation" (56).

ESSENTIAL IDEAS TO REMEMBER

Solid buildings rest upon solid foundations, crafted to an architect's carefully
calculated specifications. Undoubtedly, the firmer the foundation, the less
liable the building is to suffer damage from settling of the terrain or even
storms and natural disasters over the years.

Much like well-constructed buildings, well-constructed coaching programs are built upon solid foundations. Beginning on the right foot is crucial,
as initial first steps often set the tone for the entire endeavor. The following
key principles hold the potential to greatly assist in laying a firm foundation
for instructional technology collegial coaching programs:

- The importance of establishing coaching relationships in mutual trust,
  respect, and caring cannot be overemphasized.
- Coaches set a foundation for successful coaching experiences by learning
  more about themselves first, before seeking to guide others. Furthermore,
  effective coaches devote time to learning as much as possible about those
  they intend to coach.

- Behind every great coach is a great support system. A group of individuals that meets for the purposes of brainstorming can play a tremendous role in boosting coaches' creativity and confidence.
- When schools ensure that all communications, tools, and strategies intended to support classroom technology integration are coherent and aligned, faculty members feel better prepared to clearly formulate goals with their coaches, to more easily develop plans for achieving those goals, and to more confidently and readily proceed in that direction.
- Through teaming up with coaches and lending their vital support to coaching programs, administrators hold the potential to achieve tremendous gains in reaching and supporting teachers struggling to incorporate instructional technology.
- Cross-generational coaching can serve as an instrumental and impactful experience for coaches and coached teachers. Likenesses and differences between generations often play a beneficial and enriching role in coaching relationships.

REFERENCES

Bland, C. J., A. L. Taylor, S. L. Shollen, A. M. Weber-Main, and P. A Mulcahy. *Faculty Success through Mentoring: A Guide for Mentors, Mentees, and Leaders.* Lanham, MA: Rowman and Littlefield Education, 2009.

Dean, C. B., B. Stone, E. Hubbell, and H. Pitler. *Classroom Instruction That Works: Research-Based Strategies for Increasing Student Achievement* (2nd ed.). Alexandria, VA: ASCD, 2012.

Gardner, H. *Frames of Mind.* New York: Basic Books, 1983.

Martin, C. A., and B. Tulgan. *Managing the Generation Mix: From Collision to Collaboration.* Amherst, MA: HRD Press, 2002.

Pitler, H., E. Hubbell, M. Kuhn, and K. Malenoski. *Using Technology with Classroom Instruction That Works.* Alexandria, VA: ASCD, 2007.

Raines, C. *Connecting Generations: The Sourcebook for a New Workplace.* Menlo Park, CA: Crisp Publications, 2003.

Smith, L. *Schools That Change: Evidenced-Based Improvement and Effective Change Leadership.* Thousand Oaks, CA: Corwin Press, 2011.

Wiggins, G. P., and J. McTighe. *Understanding by Design.* Alexandria, VA: ASCD, 2005.

Chapter Seven

Acquiring Faculty Buy-In

The greatest crime in the world is not developing your potential. When you do what you do best, you are helping not only yourself, but the world.
—Roger Williams, Early English Theologian

As growing numbers of school districts busily outfit their facilities with the latest technological tools and resources, many of these substantial investments ultimately serve as nothing more than costly decor. Sadly, it is not uncommon to find computers, tablets, and others devices left to gather dust in the corners of classrooms, largely untouched and sometimes still sealed within the original packaging.

The fault lies not with the resources themselves, or even the teachers in whose rooms they take up space. Rather, it is often the methods by which they have been introduced that are to blame. Many educators who have been teaching since even before computers made their initial appearance in schools have resisted the use of technology, instead concentrating their efforts upon what they have always viewed as effective teaching.

In countless cases, such reluctant technology users are skilled and dedicated educators, many of whom inspire their students and bring about gains in learning year after year. Yet because they have not seen much impact through years of observing the latest and greatest instructional technology come and go, they feel reluctant to fix a classroom system that does not appear to be broken.

Regrettably, the bulk of professional development offered to enhance classroom technology integration seems to have been designed for technology enthusiasts rather than those reluctant to implement technological innovations. Such trainings neglect to tackle the genuine concerns of hesitant teachers. Thus, by their very nature, they fail to transform uncertainty into enthusiasm. Instead, these traditional professional development endeavors tend to heighten the eagerness of technology enthusiasts while intensifying the reservations of reluctant teachers.

Nearly anyone can recall a situation in which he or she felt a sense of hesitancy, and possibly even fear, at the thought of trying something new. As human beings anticipate the prospect of venturing out into the "great unknown"—whether in educational or career pursuits, relationships, or any number of other endeavors—the support available during critical moments in the journey can either make or break the undertaking.

Just as in any other unfamiliar experience, teachers reluctant to technology integration are inherently influenced by unique needs, interests, and learning styles. Such factors must be addressed in a respectful, intentional, and creative manner in order for these educators to embrace new technologies within their classroom learning environments. As of yet, little has been done in mainstream professional development endeavors to prepare reluctant technology users for the deluge of technological tools and resources available within today's schools.

NARROWING THE GAP

As a means of differentiating between early and late buyers of new technologies, Moore (1991) introduced the notion of a tremendous "gap" or "chasm" between these two groups of consumers. Over the years, many technology companies presumed that technology adoption (and sales) would take on a natural progression from initial enthusiasts into highly profitable later groups of consumers. Ultimately, however, this assumption led to the downfall of many once cutting-edge corporations.

In accordance with Moore's findings, the notion that late adopters naturally follow early adopters' leads has turned out to be inaccurate and risky. The process of bridging the great divide between these two groups requires a well-thought-out strategy that consists of careful consideration for divergent needs, viewpoints, and desires of late adopters. Plans that typically work well among technological forerunners will almost certainly need to be radically altered to reach late adopters.

Although the terms "early adopters" and "later adopters" originated in the technology marketplace, this analogy can be effectively applied to the varying characteristics of early and late adopters within classroom settings. Countless teachers feel reluctant to embrace technological innovation and are thus hesitant to incorporate these tools and resources into their daily teaching practices.

Yet these insights seem to have somehow eluded the world of education. One-size-fits-all professional development endeavors have essentially eradi-

cated the perception of teachers as consumers with viewpoints and preferences. Educators often unexpectedly walk into their classrooms to find new
technological tools and resources to implement without ever having re-
quested them. There is little wonder why so many of these investments go
unused.

Other notable findings from Moore's research transfer well to educational
settings. For example, late adopters desire evidence of the value of a technological tool or resource before they commit to purchasing. They expect new
technologies to generate a sizable difference in outcomes and performance.
Furthermore, they extend little patience for change and exhibit hesitancy to
modify time-tested practices without convincing proof that substantial dividends will accompany an investment of time and effort.

Additionally, late adopters desire a refined, complete product before they
purchase. They seek out user-friendly, well-supported products—the total
package. According to Moore, these types of consumers are realists, often
conventional and skeptical of any change undertaken merely for the sake of
change. They lack tolerance for half-baked, unproven methods.

Such observations regarding the marketplace also apply to myriad school
settings. As educational organizations scurry to purchase and install the latest
and greatest technological tools and resources, the widening gap between
those who embrace and those who resist such changes becomes increasingly
difficult to ignore. Furthermore, overlooking this chasm constitutes a recipe
for disaster.

Oftentimes, schools invest in only a partial product, purchasing technological infrastructure without taking the necessary steps to undergird their
most valuable asset—their human resources. Far too many educational organizations place the technological resource "cart" in front of the learning
"horse," as purchases of hardware, software, and other tools precede human
resource development.

By its highly personalized nature, collegial coaching represents an effective means of attending to the varied needs, perspectives, and learning styles
of teachers reluctant to accept technology integration. The remainder of this
chapter introduces specific, feasible steps to achieving faculty buy-in, undoubtedly among the most crucial components of effective instructional technology implementation within school settings.

TEAMWORK MAKES THE DREAM WORK

Successful coaches seek to convince their coachees that they are a part of the
same team. In coaching relationships, unity and teamwork are essential.
Whether within a school team, sports team, work team, church team, or any
other team, effective leaders ensure that everyone is aboard the bus and

traveling in the right direction. They guide and support those within their organization in realizing a common vision, focus, and purpose. In this case, the focus is on generating gains in student learning and achievement while also enhancing technology integration and 21st-century knowledge and skills.

As imperative as this goal is, anyone who has sought to build a team can attest to the fact that the process of bringing people together can be difficult. Conflicting agendas, inflated egos, power struggles, pessimism, criticism, and the absence of vision can hinder unity among team members and the ultimate success of the project.

Effective teamwork results from the dedication and engagement of school leadership and coaches in the process of building a unified team. This entails investment of focus, time, and effort, ultimately requiring that team members give greater concern to the vision and well-being of the organization than they do their personal agendas.

A transformation of thinking is fundamental. Teamwork occurs once each individual can plainly perceive how their own vision and endeavors impact the overarching vision and victory of the team. In coaching relationships, this involves meaningful words and actions initiated by the coach, thus convincing his or her coached teachers of solidarity and dedication to a team effort.

Effective coaches work shoulder-to-shoulder with coached teachers, practicing new skills and activities side by side, rather than presenting a demonstration and expecting instant duplication. Additionally, they take time to listen to the ideas of their coachees, thoughtfully reflecting upon how such suggestions might play a part in the coaching process. And successful coaches work alongside their coached teachers to transform these dreams into realities.

Furthermore, quality coaches build unified teams through laboring in the background to further their coachees' success in technology integration. Coaches dedicate the time and effort necessary to see their coachees' projects through to completion, whether this means conducting preliminary research, meeting before or staying after school to work through the kinks of implementation, standing by as a lesson is introduced to the students in order to offer support as needed, and the list goes on and on.

Additionally, successful coaches build a team-centric environment by serving as cheerleaders, offering constructive feedback and encouragement throughout the coaching endeavor. Coaches prove that they are on the same team as their coached teachers by sharing their coachees' successes—both great and small—with others in the school community.

Great coaches highlight the progress and achievements realized by their coachees while speaking with fellow faculty members and school leaders. In doing so, they convey their enthusiasm and respect for their colleagues' growth and learning endeavors. When a technology integration endeavor is successful, they find ways to share this news with as many people as possible in the school community.

As the saying goes, "You catch more flies with honey than you do with vinegar." The "honey" of heartfelt encouragement and meaningful cheerleading might just provide the impetus coached teachers need to gain newfound confidence and draw them back for additional technology integration ventures.

QUITTING IS NOT AN OPTION

Greatness is most prominently exposed when an individual perseveres in the face of tremendous challenge, beats the odds, and stands to his or her feet after rolling with the various punches life has thrown. Times like these often signify the birthplace of victory, where meaningful growth takes place.

Faculty members, like individuals within any organization, naturally feel more willing to adopt a new program or initiative when they believe they will receive adequate support along the way. The knowledge that they will have a coach to guide, uphold, and encourage them through the ups and downs of learning to implement unfamiliar technological tools and resources cannot be overemphasized.

Ultimately, coached teachers need confidence that their coaches will see them through until the end, once their integration goals have been reached, and possibly even beyond. Those involved in the program must know that quitting will not be an option—for either the coached teachers or their coaches.

In their studies of personality and adult development through coaching experiences, Susing and Cavanagh (2013) found that although effective coaching supports the practical, professional endeavors of the coachee in the shorter term, it may also positively influence adaptations in personality traits in the longer term. Perseverance in the face of trials, on the parts of both coaches and coachees, is one of the many factors of the coaching experience that can bring about such positive developmental changes, both professionally and personally.

This process, however, must be a gradual one. At first the coach should be the team member who offers to accomplish the heavy lifting. Coaches must lead by example, taking the initiative to research applicable technological tools, create learning resources, set up online accounts that might be utilized through the process, and other such foundational tasks.

In this way, coaches help prevent extra time from being taken up by tedious undertakings in the beginning stages of the program, keeping momentum high as the coachee is just commencing the process of technology implementation. Eventually, once coached teachers have witnessed the benefits of their integration endeavors, coaches can gradually release the amount of work to be done back into the teacher's hands.

ACHIEVING SMALL SUCCESSES THROUGH BABY STEPS

Effective coaches guide their coached teachers in brainstorming and planning for projects that can be quickly and easily implemented. This way, coachees can appreciate that the time spent with their coach is actually benefitting them by reducing efforts that might otherwise have been more extensive had they been left to develop such ideas on their own.

In a coaching case study, Anna, a coach on an elementary campus, assisted her coached teacher Frank in finding a website that proved integral to the development of one of his units. In commenting on his coaching experience with Anna, Frank later shared that locating this website "tipped the balance for me in using technology." After he observed how positively the students responded to the activity, he went on to independently create a website for another writing assignment.

In another example, collegial coach Lindsay worked with an entire seventh grade team to integrate technology in innovative ways as they taught a unit on Anne Frank. She reported,

> We challenged the students to create a digital background for the various scene performances they were assigned. The kids took the notion and ran with it! We saw students use sound and even create several different scenes, as opposed to just one a with a paper background. They did this by making the same picture with slight changes run at a quick speed and then running in place in front of the picture to make it look like they were really running. I think this small piece of the project really went to show just what kids will do when you open the gates for them to run free with technology. All we did was say the backgrounds could be digital, and they blew us away with their creativity and innovation.

If time and scheduling permits, an initial modeling process by the coach and observation by the coachee will likely prove very helpful. Effective technology implementation often involves adaptations to classroom seating, behavioral management, time management, and assessment practices. Allowing teachers to witness this process in action will almost certainly achieve great gains in helping them to believe in the benefits of such changes. And, ultimately, it will assist them in gaining a clearer vision for pursuing effective integration in their own classrooms.

The research of Galbraith and Anstron (1995) supports the cost-effective notion that creating a schedule that allows faculty members time for modeling and observation ultimately leads to improved teaching practices. Even if faculty members must combine classes in order to observe one another teaching both groups simultaneously, this format can still prove quite effective for providing increased opportunities for coachees to learn from watching another colleague in action.

Furthermore, it is important that coaches help coached teachers find opportunities for rapid and stress-free initial successes in their implementation. Once they see students' typically enthusiastic and engaging reactions to technology integration, coaches will likely be more apt to seek out other opportunities to integrate technology. By beginning with baby steps and building from there, coaches can effectively scaffold their coached teachers' learning experiences and pave the way for future successes with technology implementation.

CREATING AUTHENTIC COMMUNITIES OF PRACTICE

Faculty buy-in is naturally enhanced when teachers feel as though they represent an integral component of a community in which meaningful technology integration is occurring. Effective coaches strategically and reflectively seek to build communities of practice in which colleagues openly share their ideas and experiences with one another.

David, a coach on a high school campus, shared the following insights regarding a past coaching experience: "Coaching one teacher to be an incredibly efficient technology pioneer with an awesome track record only served to alienate that teacher from his horizontal team counterparts." Ultimately, David discovered that "bringing the entire horizontal team along at the same level of competency yields more than improved team dynamics. Team members are able to share experiences with each other. Their cooperation leads to more successful and meaningful application of technology."

Furthermore, David commented, "In the past, I saw horizontal teams as 'limiting' to student progress. Now though, I view the team like a sports team. They are stronger working together than as individuals. By supporting each other, accomplishments [of coached teachers] abound."

When working within a community of practice, coaches should seek out opportunities to demonstrate to their coached teachers that technology integration will almost never be seamless. Far from perfect in fact, delving into new technology implementation endeavors will often be messy. Coaches should emphasize that such outcomes are completely acceptable and even expected, finding ways to highlight the beauty in the potential chaos.

Coaches and coached teachers might need to experiment and try alternative resources, tools, and implementation strategies before deciding upon those that best address the needs of their students and campuses. Lindsay, a coach who worked with two different middle school teachers, found the following to be true:

Erik wanted to pursue incorporating Glogster [into one of his units], as he
heard Keri talking about how she used it and loved it. We created an assignment together where the students created Glogs to represent the first ten
amendments to the U.S. Constitution. The student enjoyed it much more than
traditional collage creations. Unlike Keri, Erik did not have the students
present their Glogs. Instead, they were printed and/or emailed in. He said he
may try it Keri's way next time, as he feels presenting them would be easier on
him. As he graded [the Glogs], he realized that even though the ten topics were
the same, students had lots of different illustrations that they used—and if they
used videos, then he needed to see it play (which wasn't possible as a hard
copy).

Lindsay ultimately discovered that this was a big "aha!" moment for both her
and her coached teacher Erik in regards to implementing this particular tool.
In their case, the way in which they were utilizing Glogster made a tremendous impact on the most effective plan for execution. In technology integration, as in many circumstances in life, one size very rarely fits all.

TIME: THE EVER-IMPORTANT INGREDIENT

When seeking to acquire the support of reluctant technology users, the significance of setting aside sufficient time for coaching endeavors cannot be
overstated. Debra, a coach on an elementary campus, emphasized, "Allocat-
ing time is so critical. Coaches and coachees must be dedicated to the process
and program. Developing those essential, risk-free, collaborative relationships are fundamental to a successful coaching experience. When colleagues
are not familiar with each other, building up this part can take time."
    In the words of Gladwell (2000), "If you wanted to bring about a funda-
mental change in people's beliefs and behavior—a change that will persist
and serve as an example to others—you would need to create a community
around them, where those new beliefs could be practiced and expressed and
nurtured" (173). And, as nearly anyone working within an organization can
attest, building genuine communities of practice often requires a significant
investment of time.
    Reflecting upon his own insights as a coach within a high school setting,
Nathan remarked, "When teachers volunteer to be coached and they experience results with their students, then it builds momentum for the rest of the
faculty. When teachers *choose to improve*, the outcomes are significantly
better." His experience serves as yet another powerful example of the impact
that coaching within a community can render upon faculty members' willingness to offer their full support to the program.
    Nathan also shared his findings that coaching empowers teachers to make
decisions about their classrooms. When coaching takes place within a community of practice, teachers perceive that they have a part in meaningful and

personal professional development strategies. And, naturally, it is the students who truly benefit.

Next year, Nathan will be promoted to the role of principal within his school. As such, he desires to provide the instructional support his teachers need to feel validated and successful. He also perceives the need to build internal motivation for teachers to attempt and implement innovative ideas and practices. This has all resulted from his firsthand experience with how intensely and positively coaching can influence teachers' professional practices and ultimately student learning.

ESSENTIAL IDEAS TO REMEMBER

As schools race to procure and set up the most cutting-edge technologies, the expanding chasm between those faculty members who willingly adopt and those who, either overtly or silently, struggle with such changes becomes more and more difficult to overlook. In fact, ignoring this issue can often lead to disastrous results.

Rather than investing in only a partial product by purchasing technology without taking the necessary steps to support their faculty members in effectively integrating it, today's school leaders should thoughtfully and strategically seek faculty buy-in and expertise. And collegial coaching represents a tremendous avenue through which to do so.

Support for coaching programs is naturally enhanced when faculty members feel as though coaching efforts will assist them in being part of a community of practice in which meaningful technology integration occurs. Effective coaches strategically and reflectively endeavor to create communities of practice in which colleagues openly share their ideas and experiences with one another, including both successes and failures.

Furthermore, when seeking to obtain the participation and even enthusiasm of reluctant technology users, the significance of setting aside sufficient time for coaching endeavors cannot be overstated. When coaches struggle, it is usually because of a lack of time—not a lack of willingness or expertise.

Additionally, successful coaches support their coached teachers in identifying projects that can be implemented with minimal stress and noticeable student success. This way, coachees can appreciate that the time spent with their coach benefits their teaching practice in discernible and applicable ways.

Like individuals encountering any unknown experience for the first time, teachers reluctant to integrate technology are greatly impacted by unique needs, interests, and learning styles. These considerations must be tackled in thoughtful, deliberate, and imaginative ways if hesitant faculty members are expected to welcome and utilize new technologies within their classrooms. Coaches are challenged to seek out ways of emphasizing coached teachers' strengths while stretching them individually in new ways.

Collegial coaching represents a unique means by which to address these special considerations. By its very nature, collegial coaching provides an avenue by which to deliver personalized, relevant, just-in-time support for faculty members of differing technology ability levels. Ultimately, collegial coaching offers hope to once-hesitant teachers, transforming fear into excitement as educators learn to integrate the varying tools and resources of the digital age into their professional practices.

REFERENCES

Galbraith, P., and K. Anstron. *Peer Coaching: An Effective Staff Development Model for Educators of Linguistically and Culturally Diverse Students.* Washington, DC: National Clearinghouse for Bilingual Education, 1995.

Gladwell, M. *The Tipping Point: How Little Things Can Make a Big Difference.* New York: Little Brown and Company, 2000.

Moore, G. *Crossing the Chasm.* New York: Harper Business, 1991, 2002.

Susing, I., and M. J. Cavanagh. "At the Intersection of Performance: Personality and Adult Development in Coaching," *International Coaching Psychology Review* 8(2) (2013): 58–69.

Chapter Eight

Conclusion

Continuous effort—not strength or intelligence—is the key to unlocking our potential.

—Winston Churchill

This book provides a vision and pathway whereby districts can foster an environment of collegial coaching for technology integration within educational settings. As coached teachers achieve developmental milestones, their enthusiasm often becomes contagious, thus inspiring them to share their successes with colleagues.

The transformative power of collegial coaching rests largely in its fundamental fusion of research-based, time-tested theories of teaching and learning. For example, coaching incorporates the Vygotskian concept of the Zone of Proximal Development. For decades, teachers have applied this principle in classrooms by seeking to determine not only students' current levels of functioning and potential for development in the future, but also how to most effectively support each student in grasping more advanced skills and concepts.

And this is where scaffolding comes into play. The Zone of Proximal Development represents the window between a learner's level of independent performance and the learner's level of assisted performance, or what he or she can do with support. In collegial coaching programs, coaches provide the scaffolding to connect these points, bridging the gap between a coached teacher's abilities to integrate technology independently and those skills he or she still aspires to grasp.

In addition to incorporating the Zone of Proximal Development, collegial coaching programs also assimilate reciprocal teaching, founded on Vygotsky's notion of the fundamental role of social interaction, or dialogue, in the development of cognition. According to this theory, thinking aloud and discussing ideas support illumination and revision of reasoning and learning, thereby advancing cognition. Throughout reciprocal teaching activities, appropriate support and feedback must be given to facilitate learning.

Ultimately, learning is heightened as those involved in the process take turns being the teacher. In collegial coaching, both the coach and the coachee share the roles of instructor and learner, thus allowing each to develop as educators.

WHAT'S IN A NAME?

The title of this book, *Naturalizing Digital Immigrants*, perhaps seems to suggest that this work targets a certain age group of people for technology integration—namely more senior faculty members. In actuality, through working with coaches and coachees over the years, the authors have discovered that while many younger teachers find technology integration more natural, they may not possess the content area expertise to create the most powerful technology-rich learning experiences.

On the flip side, some junior faculty members may not feel as comfortable encouraging technology access and use among students due to anticipated classroom management issues. Within the context of this book, the term "digital immigrants" applies more to teachers' digital experience than their chronological age.

Digital immigrants represent those educators who need support from experienced technology users as they attempt to meaningfully incorporate technology within their professional practices. Collegial coaching provides a professional helping relationship by which a coach can assist in whatever areas a coached teacher most needs support through this process of technology integration.

A related scenario played out very recently during a meeting of faculty members within the university at which the authors teach. Although primarily College of Education faculty members were present, the meeting was being led by a professor from the College of Business, who reported that his fellow faculty members had begun banning the use of laptops in business classes.

As one might expect, the College of Education faculty members were quite surprised at this statement! Naturally, a glaring question sprang to the minds of nearly everyone in the room: "Clearly, students will be expected to utilize computers and a wide range of technological tools within the business world. Why would anyone want to ban computers from the very classes that should be preparing them to enter, function within, and eventually impact this world?"

In questioning this faculty member, it quickly became apparent that his decision stemmed from classroom management issues. He and his colleagues felt frustrated in knowing that students might elect to use their laptops for something other than recording every word their professors spoke throughout each lesson.

Additionally, issues of pedagogy seemed to be at play. In cases in which students are not actively engaged in learning, they will find other ways to occupy their minds. Whether checking e-mails, surfing the Internet, texting, or—perhaps in cases in which technology is banned—doodling in a spiral notebook. Effective educators realize that students must be engaged! This faculty member, although highly knowledgeable about the world of business, needed some coaching in the art of teaching.

In this case, coaching represents a potential avenue through which to explore additional means of engaging students. Perhaps lecturing does not always best serve the business students within his classes. Maybe a simulation or game designed to enhance business knowledge and skills would impact students in more powerful ways than relaying a scenario from personal experience. This example offers encouragement that there is always room for improvement in the spheres of teaching and learning, no matter the experience of faculty or developmental levels of students.

The need for instructional coaches with technology expertise will only heighten as more and more technology becomes available in educational settings. In response to these developments, effective teachers will seek to plan valuable instructional pieces that allow for student-centered technology use while also building content knowledge. This goal will vary greatly from circumstance to circumstance, depending upon the students' development levels and their access to technology. The coaches' roles will fluctuate greatly as well.

As previous chapters suggest, meaningful technology integration serves to motivate and engage students in powerful ways and provides them with content area expertise. In observing the impact technology can render upon student learning experiences in classrooms, the fact remains that technology is only a tool—and not a magic wand.

Using a technological tool cannot ensure that all students will learn. However, when the RIGHT tool is utilized to teach content, this presents an opportunity for engaging teaching and deep learning to take place. For educators and learners alike, that is a beautiful thing to witness.

Creating lessons that effectively integrate technology in a natural way requires pedagogical content knowledge and technical pedagogical knowledge. As coaches begin to work with teachers, they must determine each educator's prior knowledge as it relates to technology tools, subject area content, and student expertise. The process of doing so represents a "wicked problem" entailing all kinds of variables. When the coach and coachee collaborate in planning and integration, the coached teacher benefits from being a part of the process, and the coach does as well.

YOU'VE GOT OPTIONS!

In the end, administrators must decide what type of coaching program will best address the needs of their school community. If they would like to create a more formal coaching process, then they might choose to hire a person or persons to serve as instructional coaches. Or they might decide upon a less formalized program, identifying those within the school setting to lead a peer-oriented model. Although each requires varying considerations and entails different implications, both methods can prove highly effective.

The peer-oriented model might be viewed as a "homegrown" alternative and can foster tremendous ripple effects among colleagues. In this scenario, coaches may be volunteers or hand-selected by administrators. As they work with faculty, the focus should remain on successes. Each success should be celebrated, and each celebration will result in heightened confidence in the coached teachers.

Within successful collegial coaching programs, ripple effects abound. Through triumphs great and small, coached teachers become increasingly excited about the results of their time spent with coaches. In turn, with each new success, they experience a greater desire to share their stories with others, thus becoming coaches themselves along the way.

Excellent teachers realize that meaningful learning often becomes contagious, and the learning that takes place through coaching programs is no exception. The positive ripple effects of coaching successes move through the faculty like "idea viruses"—and viruses in this case are a wonderful thing! In time, coaching may ultimately serve as a campus initiative, one from which almost everyone can benefit.

Once faculty members experience the benefits of coaching to spark brainstorming and see the power of following projects through to completion, the sky is the limit! For example, after one coached teacher experienced tremendous success in her classroom using the Web 2.0 tool Timeliner, she was asked to demonstrate the tool and share student products at her school's next faculty meeting.

In some cases, school administrators may elect to implement a more formal coaching process. In these situations, instructional coaches may be hired to facilitate quality teaching and meaningful learning with technology. In this setting, the goal for the coaches might be to help facilitate appropriate technology-rich teaching and learning (with a set number of instances per semester).

The benefits to such programs often include a more formalized assessment and reporting component. Often, since coaching involves an expense that must be accounted for, there is an additional level of accountability for the coach and those being coached. This type of program may ultimately lead to increased time and effort devoted to coaching endeavors, on the part of both coaches and coachees.

Within school settings, teachers are often tremendously pressed for time, often just "making it" from day to day. In many cases, setting aside the time to meet with coachees (especially if one person is coaching multiple colleagues), researching methods and tools by which to assist them, and supporting them through each project's completion can pose a difficult feat. However, for school campuses able to hire an instructional technologist devoted to the mission of coaching teachers in technology integration, this undertaking may be much more feasible.

REAFFIRMING THE REALITY OF SUCCESS

This guidebook closes with real-life success stories involving the transformation of teacher technology integration through collegial coaching, designed to inspire and inform readers in their journey to implement this strategy within their own professional settings. Such narratives serve to reaffirm the reality that an investment in coaching through successful technology integration holds the potential to profoundly and perpetually transform the culture of a campus.

In the authors' own experiments with over sixty-five different campuses with collegial coaches, they have witnessed success after success. The following statements represent some of the coached teachers' personal testimonials after participating in a semester-long coaching experience:

- "My students were engaged, and authentic application and evaluation were truly happening in my classroom."
- "I am finally beginning to see how technology is not just an extra burden, but a fun and meaningful tool to help kids learn content."
- "This experience was very streamlined and well organized, making it easy to work with my coach to integrate these new tools into my classroom."
- "Technology coaching has opened my eyes to the possibility of improving my methods in the classroom. I also realize how much the students enjoy using it. Allowing students complete access for assessments is a positive change of pace from in-class paper/pencil assessments."
- "I liked the hands-on ability to see the tool in use, and then being able to practice it."

And below are several quotes from the coaches themselves regarding their experiences with coaching fellow faculty members:

- "The best thing about coaching for technology integration is the fluid concept for both the mentor and coach. It allows each teacher to grow at a pace he/she is comfortable with, while challenging each in a fun and comfortable manner. Barriers are reduced and comfort levels rise, allowing creativity to bloom."
- "Technology integration does not happen from a helpdesk."
- "This experience also opened my eyes to how valuable collegial coaching is as compared to the traditional professional development that teachers are required to complete today. In this process, not only does a teacher have one point of contact for questions, issues, concerns, and ideas, but they also get the chance to try things in their classroom in a real-time basis rather than having to wait until the school year starts to try something. That is not to say that the traditional professional development is a thing of the past, but it might be most appropriate when used in combination with a collegial coaching model."
- "I truly believe the coaching process is the most effective form of professional development. Every learner, no matter what age, benefits when instruction is personalized, supportive, and tailored to meet the learner's specific needs. Schools that utilize technology coaches will see an increase in teacher and student achievement in a shorter period of time than schools that simply rely on standard professional development."
- "I would recommend educators or administrators who want to increase the technology use in their school to consider using individualized coaching rather than faculty-wide professional development. There are a few individuals who will implement a new technology after brief exposure to it, but I think the majority of teachers require additional prompting and individualization before they realize how effective the technology could be in their classrooms. From my coaching experience, I learned change in an individual takes time. I think relationship, accountability, and an ability to individualize technology to fit specific personality types and content is essential for a coach."
- "In my role as instructional technologist, I have decided to drop my 'Tech Tuesdays' in lieu of more lucrative content knowledge oriented individual coaching."

ESSENTIAL IDEAS TO REMEMBER

In order for anyone to find success in coaching endeavors, he or she must understand and accept that coaching takes time. Both coaches and coachees must be willing to devote time to see projects through to completion, to reach set goals, and to realize meaningful and lasting benefits from the experience.

Teachers and coaches must carve out time to meet together for planning (often before or after school or during their conference periods), time to do research, and time to develop teaching resources. This will not always be an easy process, but the time and efforts devoted are well worth the investment when students' engagement and learning are heightened.

Technological developments will not likely diminish, and with each new innovation, students will grow increasingly interested in the vast potential technology offers for supporting them in creating, critical thinking, communicating, and collaborating. In an ever-changing world, educators must learn to adapt their thinking and professional practices in order to reach their students at their points of interest and engagement. Otherwise, they run the risk of losing them altogether.

Through the last several years, many schools have experienced great struggle with technology integration. These challenges are often magnified as the latest and greatest technologies are purchased without an investment in the most valuable resources a school as to offer—its human resources.

Actions must be taken to address every teacher's need to be empowered, not overwhelmed. Collegial coaching addresses this need by enabling both educators and students to embrace the potential of technology, ultimately becoming 21st-century learners and innovators.

Lightning Source UK Ltd.
Milton Keynes UK
UKHW011120120919
349641UK00010B/21/P

9 781475 812817